Lecture Notes in Computer Science

Commenced Publication in 1973
Founding and Former Series Editors:
Gerhard Goos, Juris Hartmanis, and Jan van Leeuwen

Sven van der Meer   Mark Burgess
Spyros Denazis (Eds.)

Modelling Autonomic Communications Environments

Third IEEE International Workshop, MACE 2008
Samos Island, Greece, September 22-26, 2008
Proceedings

 Springer

Volume Editors

Sven van der Meer
Waterford Institute of Technology (WIT)
Telecommunications Software & Systems Group (TSSG)
Cork Road, Waterford, Ireland
E-mail: vdmeer@tssg.org

Mark Burgess
University College Oslo
Faculty of Engineering
P.O.Box 4, St Olavs Plass, 0130 Oslo, Norway
E-mail: burgess@iu.hio.no

Spyros Denazis
University of Patras
Department of Electrical and Computer Engineering, 26504 Rio, Greece
E-mail: sdena@ece.upatras.gr

Library of Congress Control Number: Applied for

CR Subject Classification (1998): C.2, C.2.3, F.1.1, D.4.1, D.4.4

LNCS Sublibrary: SL 5 – Computer Communication Networks
and Telecommunications

ISSN 0302-9743

ISBN 978-3-540-87354-9 Springer Berlin Heidelberg New York

Springer is a part of Springer Science+Business Media

springer.com

© Springer-Verlag Berlin Heidelberg 2008

Typesetting: Camera-ready by author, data conversion by Scientific Publishing Services, Chennai, India
Printed on acid-free paper   SPIN: 12523726   06/3180   5 4 3 2 1 0

Preface

Research and development of autonomics have come a long way, and we are delighted to present the proceedings of the *3rd IEEE International Workshop on Modelling Autonomic Communications Environments (MACE 2008)*. As in the last two years, this workshop was held as part of Manweek, the International Week on Management of Networks and Services, which took place on the lovely Island of Samos in Greece.

MACE started as an experiment in 2006, and created a small community that now finds itself attracted back each year by a feeling of excitement – that there is something new going on. Certainly, MACE is not as shiny or practiced as other well-known conferences and workshops, but we consider this a feature of the workshop itself. New ideas, a little rough around the edges (and sometimes more than a little), often quite unfinished, pop out and provoke extensive discussion. Science needs this kind of exploratory adventure and we were strongly motivated to preserve this atmosphere of exploration and discussion in this year's program. It is also very interesting to observe the support of industry for MACE, indicating that there is a need for new ideas outside the classical academic circles.

This year, the submissions were more peripheral to the invited themes of the workshop than in the last two years. We saw prototypes emerging and experiments maturing that attempt to now employ the principles introduced in previous years. We can call this part of MACE the "protoautonomics," acknowledging that we still have some way to go, but that we are at the exciting beginning of the journey.

The book you are holding in your hands presents the accepted papers of the technical sessions of MACE 2008. We had 22 submissions, of which 8 were accepted as full papers. Furthermore, we allowed four submissions as short papers. To make sure that the accepted papers provide an interesting program, we discussed all the submissions and all the reviews provided by the MACE TPC in full detail. We believe that, to support the objectives of MACE, this effort was well-worth doing and we hope that this book provides you with cutting-edge ideas, thoughtfully presented solutions and pursuable experiments.

We are very proud to present this year's proceedings as a volume of Springer's *Lecture Notes in Computer Science (LNCS)*. The volume contains four chapters. We start by looking at "Autonomic Networks, Experiences and Frameworks", presenting the results of two European projects in terms of experiments for application development and in-network management. The second chapter – "Strategies, Processes and Generation of Components" – provides a sophisticated insight of algorithms underpinning the realization of autonomic networks. The third chapter is dedicated to discussions on "Self-* Capabilities," focusing on self-healing, self-organizing and self-management. The fourth and last chapter comprises our "Short Papers," looking at information models, domain-specific models, negotiation and models for the provision of services in autonomic communication environments.

As in the last years, MACE was part of Manweek, an umbrella of now six workshops and conferences focusing on different aspects of network and service management, from distributed operations (DSOM) via IP-based management (IPOM) towards multimedia and mobile networks (MMNS), virtualization (EVGM) and middleware for next-generation networks (NGNM). Further information of Manweek and the individual workshops and conferences can be found at http://www.manweek.org.

Finally, we would like to thank the many people whose hard work and commitment were essential to the success of MACE 2008. Foremost amongst these are the researchers who submitted papers to the workshop. We would like to express our gratitude to the MACE Technical Program Committee for their advice and support through all the stages of the workshop preparation. We thank all reviewers for their fair and helpful reviews. We thank IEEE Communications Society and the Autonomic Communications Forum (AFC) for support and sponsorship of MACE. Most of the more time-consuming practical and logistical organization tasks for the workshop were handled by the members of the Manweek 2008 Organization Committee – this made our jobs significantly easier, and for that we are very grateful. Finally, we wish to acknowledge the financial support of the Manweek sponsors, whose contributions were hugely instrumental in helping us run what we hope was a stimulating, rewarding and, most importantly, an enjoyable workshop for all its participants.

September 2008   Sven van der Meer
                                                          Mark Burgess
                                                         Spyros Denazis

MACE 2008 Organization

Workshop and Program Co-chairs

Sven van der Meer   Waterford Institute of Technology, Ireland
Mark Burgess   University College Oslo, Norway
Spyros Denazis   University of Patras, Greece

Steering Committee

John Strassner   Motorola, USA
Willie Donnelly   Waterford Institute of Technology, Ireland
Brendan Jennings   Waterford Institute of Technology, Ireland

Publication Chair

Tom Pfeifer   Waterford Institute of Technology, Ireland

Publicity Co-chair

Luciano Paschoal Gaspary   Universidade Federal do Rio Grande do Sul, Brazil

Treasurers

Sofoklis Kyriazakos   Converge, Greece
Brendan Jennings   Waterford Institute of Technology, Ireland

Website and Registration Chair

Sven van der Meer   Waterford Institute of Technology, Ireland

Submission Chair

Lisandro Granville   Universidade Federal do Rio Grande do Sul, Brazil

Sponsoring Co-chairs

E. Pallis   Centre for Technological Research of Crete,
                                     Greece
I. Venieris   National Technical University of Athens,
                                     Greece

Manweek 2008 Chair

George Kormentzas   University of the Aegean, Greece

Manweek 2008 Vice Chair

Francisco Guirao   European Commission

Manweek 2008 Advisors

Raouf Boutaba   University of Waterloo, Canada
Brendan Jennings   Waterford Institute of Technology, Ireland
Sven van der Meer   Waterford Institute of Technology, Ireland

MACE 2008 Technical Program Committee

Nazim Agoulmine   Université d'Evry, France
Nancy Alonistioti   University of Athens, Greece
Demissie Aredo   University College Oslo, Norway
Alessandro Bassi   Hitachi Sophia Antipolis Lab, France
Robin Braun   University of Technology, Sydney, Australia
Mark Burgess   University College Oslo, Norway
Monique Calisti   Whitestein Technologies, Switzerland
Greg Cox   Motorola Labs, USA
Filip De Turck   University of Ghent, Belgium
Spyros Denazis   University of Patras, Greece
Willie Donnelly   Waterford Institute of Technology, Ireland
Joel Fleck II.   Hewlett-Packard, USA
Yacine Ghamri-Doudane   Institut d'Informatique d'Entreprise, France
Brendan Jennings   Waterford Institute of Technology, Ireland
George Karetsos   Teilar, Greece
Ahmed Karmouch   University of Ottawa, Canada
Dave Lewis   Trinity College Dublin, Ireland
Sven van der Meer   Waterford Institute of Technology, Ireland
Kinji Mori   TiTech, Japan
Maurice Mulvenna   Ulster University, UK
Tadashi Nakano   University of California, Irvine, USA
José Neuman de Souza   Federal University of Caera, Brazil

Giorgio Nunzi	NEC Europe, Germany
Mícheál Ó Foghlú	Waterford Institute of Technology, Ireland
Declan O'Sullivan	Trinity College Dublin, Ireland
Manish Parashar	Rutgers University, USA
Dave Raymer	Motorola Labs, USA
Fabio Ricciato	The Telecommunications Research Center Vienna, Austria
Mikhail Smirnov	Fraunhofer FOKUS, Germany
Roy Sterritt	University of Ulster, UK
John Strassner	Motorola Labs, USA
James Won-Ki Hong	POSTECH, Korea
Mazin Yousif	Avirtec, USA

Additional Reviewers

Apostolis Koussaridas	University of Athens, Greece
Costas Polychronopoulos	University of Athens, Greece
Nancy Samaan	University of Ottawa, Canada

Table of Contents

Autonomic Networks, Experiences and Frameworks

Strategies, Processes and Generation of Components

Self-* Capabilities

Short Papers, Early Work and Applied Studies

Experiences with Application Development for Autonomic Networks

Karl-André Skevik, Matti Siekkinen, Vera Goebel, and Thomas Plagemann

Department of Informatics, University of Oslo
P.O. Box 1080 Blindern, N-0316 Oslo, Norway
{karlas,siekkine,goebel,plageman}@ifi.uio.no

Abstract. ANA is a project that examines legacy-free future networking architectures, with a focus on autonomicity. The programming model used in ANA dispenses with the rigid layers of the OSI model and instead uses *bricks* that can be combined to build a *compartment* offering the functionality required by an application. Restrictions such as TCP always being layered on top of IP do not exist, with e.g., arbitrary bricks offering transport functionality being usable to communicate with other nodes in a compartment. Application functionality is divided among specialized bricks, giving a clean and non-monolithic design. We have designed a P2P-like distributed streaming system from scratch, and designed an information sharing system by adapting an existing structured P2P system for ANA. In this paper, we report our experiences on the benefits and pitfalls of application and service development for ANA, and draw some conclusions on suitable design approaches for such novel "disruptive" network architectures.

1 Introduction

Research work on autonomic computing systems has originally been motivated by the effort and complexity of configuration, management, and maintenance of the continuously increasing number of networked computing systems that exist today. The advantage of autonomic networks is obvious in the area of network management because they minimize manual intervention. Making networks autonomic by introducing self-* properties is one of the key elements in many of the recent efforts towards the future Internet, like ANA [1], BIONETS, and CASCADAS[1]. While the challenges of autonomic network solutions receive a strong attention in the research community, little effort has so far been put into the investigation of distributed applications using autonomic networks. Even if self-* properties are introduced into the network, these properties themselves should not be the ultimate goal; instead, the added value of autonomic networks should ultimately be benefits provided to end-users, applications, and application developers.

In order to understand the challenges and benefits that application developers are confronted with when implementing applications for autonomic networks, we

---

[1] www.ana-project.org, www.bionets.eu, www.cascadas-project.org

S. van der Meer, M. Burgess, and S. Denazis (Eds.): MACE 2008, LNCS 5276, pp. 1–13, 2008.

analyze in this paper two complementary cases of application development in the ANA Project (Autonomic Networking Architecture). The ANA Project is pursuing disruptive research towards solutions for the future Internet. Besides the development of networking concepts with self-* properties, ANA has introduced an abstract notion of communication starting points to enable the construction of ANA networks without limitations on addressing mechanisms. Furthermore, ANA uses the concepts of compartments composed of smaller bricks to build systems that offer services or application functionality. Each brick offers a simple service and can be used in multiple compartments.

Since ANA does not have a strict layering, like in the OSI reference model, the boundary between network, overlay, and application is fuzzy. Each of these are in fact represented by a compartment. Even all functional blocks running on a node form a compartment. In this paper, we use the term application for the "higher" layer compartments that offer functionality that would be implemented as overlays or applications in a layered architecture. The common factor for these application compartments is that they might need the services of some basic network compartments, such as an IP compartment, for example.

Based on these fundamental concepts, we have designed and implemented two applications: a Peer-to-Peer (P2P) video-on-demand streaming system and a Multi-Compartment Information Sharing System (MCIS) which is essentially a structured P2P system. The P2P streaming system is based on our earlier research on P2P based streaming [2], but the architecture and code has been redesigned from scratch to make use of ANA concepts in order to benefit from the advantages of autonomic networks. In contrast to this fully redesigned system, with the MCIS implementation we have tried to reuse the open source *Mercury* system [3] as much as possible; the MCIS implementation represents the approach of porting legacy applications and overlays to a new autonomic networking architecture. The contribution of this work is a description and analysis of the experiences and tradeoffs of porting versus redesigning and reimplementing applications for future autonomic networks.

Section 2 introduces relevant ANA concepts and gives a short overview of the fundamental APIs used by ANA developers. Section 3 describes MCIS and the process of adapting it for ANA. Section 4 presents the design of a streaming compartment developed for ANA. Section 5 concludes this article with a summary of our contributions.

2   A Glimpse of the ANA Architecture

The objective of the ANA project is a clean slate design of a network architecture for the future Internet with an autonomic flavor. The ANA approach is disruptive in that it does not build on top of the current Internet. Instead, ANA defines a small set of abstractions that form the basic building blocks of the architecture, and that make it possible to host, federate, and interconnect an arbitrary number of heterogeneous networks. These abstractions are *Information Channel (IC)*, *Information Dispatch Point (IDP)*, *Functional Block (FB)*, and *Compartment*.

Protocols and algorithms are represented as FBs in ANA. These FBs can be composed together in any desired manner to produce a specific packet processing functional chain. Communication in ANA occurs towards the start point (the IDP) of a communication channel (the IC). FBs send messages to IDPs which are dispatch points for the next FB. This mechanism makes it possible to recompose the functional chain that represents a specific IC at run time, which is necessary for the control loop behavior of an autonomic system.

A network is represented as a compartment in ANA. ANA does not mandate anything about the internals of a specific compartment, which is free to define inter-compartment communication parameters such as naming, addressing, and routing. Instead, ANA specifies how these compartments interact by introducing a generic compartment API. This API consists of five basic primitives: publish(), unpublish(), resolve(), lookup(), and send(). The implementation of this API represents the external interface of a compartment. The underlying idea is that a service (represented as a FB) is able to publish itself within a compartment. Users of that service (other FBs) are able to resolve a communication channel (an IC) to the service via that compartment, after which they can send data to each other. An analogy to the layered architecture used today would be an IP FB publishing itself to be reachable at a specific IP address within an Ethernet compartment, enabling other IP FBs to resolve (using the published IP address) an IC to that IP FB via the Ethernet compartment. In addition, compartments can look up specific kinds of services based on keywords if it is not exactly known what to resolve.

The programming model used in ANA is based on *bricks*. There are two kinds of bricks: those that offer access to a network protocol compartment, and those that implement operations such as caching or encryption. Application functionality is divided among specialized bricks, giving a clean and non-monolithic design. A more detailed overview of ANA internals can be found at the ANA web site[2].

The abstractions described above form the blueprint for the architecture and are merely the tools that enable autonomic operations. Establishment of self-* properties naturally requires additional development of corresponding services, such as those that provide resilience or functional recomposition, for instance. Furthermore, various support services are needed, among which one of the most crucial is monitoring services; knowing the current state is imperative for autonomic behavior.

3   MCIS: Multi-Compartment Information Sharing System

For an autonomic network, a generic and fully distributed information sharing service is needed to disseminate monitoring information for decision making. The Multi-Compartment Information Sharing System (MCIS) offers this, by providing lookup and storage facilities for any client brick wishing to share data with other

---

[2] http://www.ana-project.org/web/meetings/start

bricks. The system is rich in capabilities and supports range queries over multi-attribute data records, publish/subscribe functionality, and one-time queries.

3.1   Design and Implementation

In order to create an information sharing service for ANA, we have used an already existing open source system called Mercury [3]. Mercury is a structured P2P system where nodes are logically organized on a ring, in a way similar to Chord [4]. The key difference is that Mercury does not hash the keys, which are the actual attribute values. Hence, each node in the ring is responsible for a particular attribute value range. This difference makes it possible to process range queries efficiently. In Mercury the rings are called attribute hubs and there is one hub for each attribute of a data record. For example, if the data records are two-dimensional coordinates with x and y values as attributes, then Mercury will maintain two attribute hubs and each node is responsible for a particular value range in both of the hubs. Data records are replicated and routed to each of the hubs while queries are routed only to the hub of the attribute that is estimated to be most selective in the query predicate (i.e. specifies the smallest range). This

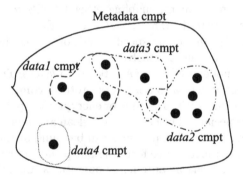

Fig. 1. Data compartments in MCIS

kind of content addressable overlay fits well to the concept of a compartment in ANA. All data records of a specific type naturally forms a *data compartment*. Each data compartment routes messages via its attribute hubs independently of other data compartments. Resolution and publish procedures of data items boil down to query processing and store operations, respectively. There is a special *metadata compartment* which every node belongs to. It contains information about the different data compartments that exist and enables discovery of them (see Figure 1). As the name suggests, the MCIS brick is the entry point to the data compartments and handles all the resolve, lookup, and publish requests from local client bricks. MCIS bricks at different nodes cooperate on the maintenance of a single distributed Mercury system per data compartment.

The Mercury software has been designed in a very modular way. The code for the overlay management and routing is located in the mercury package, while code for the underlay networking layer can be found in packages such as *wan-env* for TCP/UDP communication over IP using the Berkeley sockets API. Establishing point-to-point communication with other nodes in ANA requires being able to resolve the other end point via some compartment, where that end point has previously published itself. Thus, we needed to implement *ana-env* as the underlying ANA networking layer. Ideally this layer would choose, from the available network compartments, one that is most suitable for reaching a particular end point in the current situation. However, in the current implementation the network compartment must be chosen with a parameter when the system is started.

In addition to the networking layer, we needed to build the MCIS brick functionality; the handling of the resolve, lookup, and publish requests as specified by the generic compartment API. The brick functionality can be seen as a kind of adaptation layer, from the generic compartment API to the Mercury specific API and message types.

3.2   Lessons Learned

One particularly cumbersome issue we had in incorporating Mercury into ANA was the use of identifiers. ANA as a "disruptive" future networking architecture does not mandate the use of IP or any other protocol for communication, while the current Internet makes almost exclusive use of IP. As a consequence, as with most software designed for the Internet, Mercury assumes the use of IP addresses and port numbers as identifiers of services and clients. As a consequence, we needed to modify major parts of the entire source code to introduce strings as generic identifiers.

The main reason why it has been quite straightforward to use Mercury as the basis for building the MCIS brick has been the modularity of the source code. While it likely stems from the fact that the authors of the original code wanted to use a simulated networking layer in addition to the sockets API. Apart from the changes needed to support more generic identifiers, this separation between network layers enabled us to use the original code with only minor modifications.

Our work on Mercury has shown how porting legacy Internet networking software to ANA with only a minimum of modifications can be done, but there is still room for further integration. The original software could be decomposed into smaller consistent functionalities, which could then serve in several contexts. For example, the load balancing functionality of Mercury might also be usable by other compartments.

4   Streaming Compartment Design

For real-time applications such as video streaming systems, having accurate information about the network, such as delay or available bandwidth between nodes, can be an important factor in achieving good performance. Unfortunately, this kind of information is not easily obtainable on the current Internet. Several techniques for doing this, such as [5], have been proposed, but while it is possible to keep code for this kind of functionality in an external library rather than inside the application, the underlying limitations do not change: the Internet does not provide an interface for obtaining all the information required by the application, and a library might require updates as the interconnect technologies of the Internet changes.

However, in ANA, monitoring is provided as a fundamental service on all nodes. Furthermore, ANA has been designed to support having accurate information provided by routers and other intermediate nodes. As we have previously designed a P2P video streaming system for the Internet [2], we have been interested in seeing how having the monitoring services available in ANA might affect the design of a similar system.

4.1   Compartment Overview

We have designed a distributed compartment that offers video streaming services, with content retrievable from participating nodes that have previously retrieved the same content. This kind of system requires a mechanism for transmitting media data between nodes, but also a metadata handling system that offers file search functionality and a way of keeping track of the nodes that have copies of the data. A typical usage scenario would be for a user to search for and request a movie, upon which a list of nodes with the content available would be obtained, and the content requested from nodes on the list. The downloaded parts of the movie would simultaneously be made available to other users. Files are divided into blocks to make information about downloaded files easier to share and manage.

Some functionality is clearly the same regardless of whether an application has been designed for the Internet or ANA; disk caching and media playback occurs after the media data has been retrieved from the network and can be identical. What reveals the special characteristics of ANA is how the application is structured. A typical Internet application use have a *poll()* loop, or multiple threads, to multiplex connections to other nodes, but it is common to have the majority of the functionality implemented as part of a single application, perhaps even running as a single process. If there is any code shared between applications, it is primarily in the form of shared libraries that implement common operations.

Rather than building monolithic applications, the ANA application development concept is based on the principle of combining many small *bricks* to form a larger structure, or compartment, that offers application functionality. This might seem similar to the use of libraries, but a brick is an actively running service that can be included in the combined structure of multiple compartments. As with libraries, this gives the benefit of sharing code, but there are additional benefits that come from bricks being a running and shared service. The first is with regard to efficiency, especially in the context of network monitoring. An Internet application that wishes to estimate the transfer speed or available bandwidth to another node can do this by transmitting specially crafted packets [5], but if each application does this independently the result will be redundant traffic that increases the load on the link between the two machines needlessly. However, if all applications request this information through the same brick, the result will be less overhead and shorter response time if the answer is already known. Another important benefit comes from the possibility for the application to adapt to changes; the system can react to changes in the network by changing the bricks that offer various types of functionality. To use the network monitoring example, on the Internet, it might only be possible to use heuristics to estimate link speeds and a monitoring brick for the Internet would use these kinds of techniques, but on a network where ANA nodes provide additional monitoring functionality, the routers can be queried directly. An ANA node can react to these two different scenarios by replacing the relevant monitoring brick. The design of ANA gives applications the inherent possibility of having this kind of adaptability, and this approach can be used in many situations: in order to change transport protocols, insertion of transcoding bricks to reduce media size on low bit rate links, etc.

The use of bricks has a direct influence on the structure of the application; the streaming functionality is not offered by a single brick, but by a set of bricks that work together. One immediate benefit of this is that some of the required functionality is already offered by the system; network monitoring is provided by the monitoring framework. What remains is a way to exchange media data, metadata handling, and the interface to the media player. To demonstrate the flexibility of the brick system, we have designed two variants of the streaming system. The first is server based and similar to a traditional video streaming system suited for commercial streaming, with data originating from a server maintained by a content provider. The server also provides metadata handling services such as file search. The difference from a traditional client/server system is that clients serve downloaded content to other clients; the server is the origin

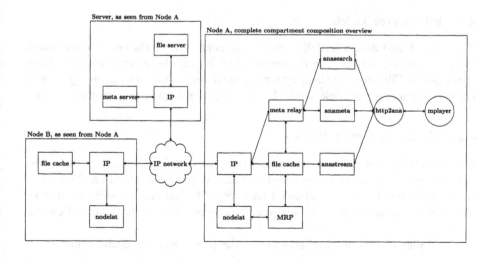

Fig. 2. Server based streaming compartment

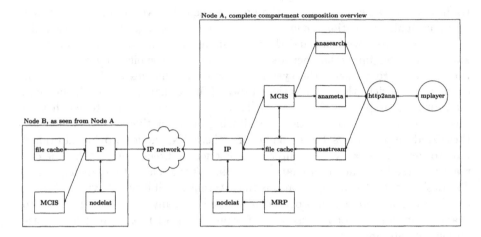

Fig. 3. Distributed streaming compartment

of all content, but not necessarily the only location to retrieve media data from. The structure of this variant is shown in Figure 2.

The second variant is a completely distributed system, with no centralized servers. Any user can publish files, resulting in a system similar to P2P file sharing networks such as eDonkey [6]. The decentralization is achieved through the use of the MCIS brick, which provides metadata handling. The structure of this system is given in Figure 3, and as can be seen, despite being two completely different systems, the only difference in the brick composition of *Node A* is that the brick managing metadata has been replaced; the rest of the system is identical.

4.2   File Server Brick

The server based design initially provides all content from the server maintained by the content provider. The *file server brick* handles byte-range requests from client nodes. Files are identified by a message digest, which is obtained by clients through the metadata brick. An IP brick is used for communication with clients.

4.3   Metadata Server Brick

Metadata in the server based streaming compartment is managed by the *metadata server brick*. For this usage scenario all files are maintained on the server; users can report having downloaded parts of a file, but cannot add new files to the system. Metadata queries only search metadata for the files located on the server.

The design of this brick reflects one of the places where a decision had to be taken with regard to the granularity of bricks. The brick performs tasks relevant for a single type of operation, namely metadata management, but there are two types of metadata: the digest, node, block, 3-tuple, and the information relevant for media files, such as movie title and quality. An alternative approach would have been to have two bricks instead of one, and it is conceivable that either brick would be useful by itself for other compartments. In general, the two opposite extremes for brick design is to have either a small number of complex bricks, or a large number of small atomic bricks. The first results in code complexity, while the second increases system complexity. We have chosen a solution in the middle, with bricks divided based on the conceptual operation they provide, rather than the low-level operation they perform.

4.4 File Cache Brick

The *file cache brick* is an important part of both the server based and distributed system. As the brick composition overview of either system shows, this is the most connected brick, with communication links to four other bricks. The task of this brick is to manage the file cache on end user nodes. This includes managing the file data stored on disk, and retrieving missing data from either the file cache or file server brick on other nodes.

As with the metadata server brick, this brick performs multiple tasks that could have been implemented in separate bricks. For example, answering data requests from remote and local nodes could have been done by two different bricks. The same is the case with the data retrieval functionality. In practice however, it was found that all these operations were quite tightly connected, and having them in separate bricks would have required synchronization mechanisms to ensure safe handling of the data stored on disk and in memory, adding complexity and essentially defeating the purpose of separating the bricks.

4.5 Meta Relay and MCIS

In both the server based and distributed streaming scenarios, the metadata requests pass through a single block. In the server case, this is the *meta relay block*, which simply relays all requests to or from the meta server block on the server node. Because of this, the interface is essentially the same as that given for the meta server brick, except that the brick is not available through the IP compartment, only to the bricks on the same node. When the MCIS is used for metadata handling, the metadata requests are processed in the context of the MCIS compartments. Support for other ways of managing metadata can be added by simply writing a new brick that supports the same interface as these two bricks.

4.6 Application Bricks

The three application bricks, *anasearch*, *anameta*, and *anastream*, have been designed to be used as normal shell commands, and each provide a simple interface to the ANA streaming system. Of these commands, anasearch and anameta are simply wrappers around the meta brick, allowing a user to search for and obtain information about available files. The anastream brick returns a media data stream for a specified file.

Again, also in this case it would have been possible to handle the brick division in a different way. Metadata queries are performed by two bricks; *anastream* and *anameta*, and the functionality of these bricks could arguably have been implemented in a single brick. The reason for the division in this case is that integrating ANA bricks with the UNIX shell is currently somewhat cumbersome, and keeping the two metadata query types in different commands makes it possible to have more easily understandable interfaces for the commands.

4.7   HTTP Proxy Based ANA Gateway

The *http2ana* and *mplayer* elements in Figure 2 and Figure 3 are not ANA bricks but standard UNIX applications. To demonstrate that ANA can be used with a normal media player, we have created a gateway application that functions as a normal HTTP proxy, that, rather than obtaining data from a web server, uses the application bricks to retrieve the data over an ANA network. Any media player that supports streaming over HTTP, and has support for HTTP proxies, should be usable with this gateway.

4.8   Non-compartment Bricks

The core part of the streaming functionality is provided by the file cache brick and the metadata handling bricks, but network monitoring is important for performance reasons, and node monitoring functionality is provided by the MRP brick[7]. The information provided by the MRP brick includes simple status information such as whether a node is available or not, but can include more complex queries such as a request for an ordering of the nodes based on criteria such as latency.

MRP operations manipulate so-called *nodesets*, that can consist of an arbitrary set of nodes. Operations include adding nodes to a nodeset, removing nodes, and requesting orderings of the nodes based on various criteria. The MRP brick does not perform any measurement operations itself, it merely manages a set of nodes, and sends requests for network measurements to the monitoring framework, here represented by the *nodelat brick*. This brick measures the RTT between the node itself and a different node. Each nodelat brick currently exposes the latency measurement interface to other bricks on the same node, but it would be possible to expose it to other nodes, allowing these nodes to measure the RTT between arbitrary sets of nodes.

The final brick which is part of the streaming compartment is the IP brick, which provides IP transport functionality.

4.9   Lessons Learned and Limitations

The current status of the streaming compartment is that all the bricks needed for the server based scenario have been implemented and are currently undergoing testing. During the development process we have made several observations. We have especially found that the brick concept leads itself well to easy development and code testing. Most bricks are fairly small and provide a single operation through a well-defined interface. The brick based application construction encourages having small bricks that are simple and consequently, ideally easy to understand and test. Compared to the development of the P2P video streaming system we have previously created for the Internet, it has been much simpler to develop and test multiple separate bricks than one large application. It should be noted that the Internet application was more feature rich, but changing the brick based design is much simpler, as can be seen in the ease with which the structure of the system is changed from being server based to being fully distributed, by simply using a different brick for metadata handling. Furthermore, having a monitoring framework has made it possible to add network awareness without having to implement code for this in the application.

While the underlying principles of ANA provide several benefits for application design, there are some practical issues that have affected brick development. The ANA project looks at legacy-free networking design, and a consequence of this is that functionality that is taken for granted on the Internet needs to be reimplemented from scratch. As the ANA code base is still far from mature, there are some limitations that have influenced the design. One obvious oddity is the use of IP to transport media data, and the system does in fact do streaming directly on top of IP packets. The reason for this is that there are currently no higher level protocols implemented; only Ethernet and IP transport without packet fragmentation. The consequence is that as opposed to having a simple stream-like interface, the bricks need to consider factors such as packet size .All requests and replies are currently kept below the MTU, which complicates request handling. Lack of a reliable transport protocol makes it necessary to handle retransmission of lost packets in the application. However, these limitations should disappear as more advanced bricks become available. It could rather be argued that these limitations demonstrate the flexibility of ANA, as it is possible to implement a distributed streaming system on top of a simple IP implementation. The functionality offered by the MRP brick is similarly limited due to the lack of network measurement bricks.

5   Conclusion

In this article, we have described work on application development in the context of ANA. A central ANA concept is the separation of functionality into bricks that offer a single type of service, and the combination of bricks to form compartments that offer more complex functionality. We have shown how this approach affects both the porting of the MCIS information sharing system to ANA, and the development from scratch of a distributed video streaming system. There are still limitations that complicate application development, but these issues are a result of functionality that has still not been implemented rather than limitations imposed by the design of ANA. More than being a deficiency, being able to do streaming directly over IP demonstrates the flexibility of ANA. Our experience shows that the brick concept is well suited for application development.

Furthermore, we have shown that the ANA compartment concept fits with currently used networking paradigms, using a content addressable network in the form of data compartments. Importing legacy software can be straightforward but usually requires a kind of adaptation layer in order to conform to the generic compartment API. A complicating factor can be the implicit assumption of IP addresses as locators and identifiers in existing application design. Such design decision often influence the entire source code and, therefore, require modifications throughout the code of a legacy application when imported to an identifier/locator agnostic environment.

There are many similarities between the brick concept and the use of shell commands in UNIX. If bricks could be combined in an easy way similar to shell commands, with a language designed for this purpose, it would make the brick concept even more powerful, and simplify the creation of complex networking applications. Especially important in this context is the existence of a monitoring framework, which can be assumed to exist on any ANA node, and which allows easy integration of monitoring operations into a compartment.

As for future work, it consists of two directions of research. First, to complete testing and integration of the compartment. Second, to further examine the applicability of the brick concept to application development, by trying to identify basic functionality that is common to many applications, and how these can be interfaced via a high-level shell-like language.

Acknowledgment. This work has been funded by the EC-funded ANA Project (FP6-IST-27489), and supported by the CONTENT Network-of-Excellence.

References

1. Jelger, C., Tschudin, C.F., Schmid, S., Leduc, G.: Basic abstractions for an autonomic network architecture. In: WoWMoM 2007: Proceedings of the 2007 International Symposium on a World of Wireless, Mobile and Multimedia Networks (2007)
2. Skevik, K.A.: The SPP architecture – A system for interactive Video-on-Demand streaming. PhD thesis, University of Oslo (April 2007)
3. Bharambe, A.R., Agrawal, M., Seshan, S.: Mercury: supporting scalable multi-attribute range queries. In: SIGCOMM 2004: Proceedings of the 2004 conference on Applications, technologies, architectures, and protocols for computer communications, pp. 353–366. ACM Press, New York (2004)
4. Stoica, I., Morris, R., Karger, D., Kaashoek, M.F., Balakrishnan, H.: Chord: A scalable peer-to-peer lookup service for internet applications. In: SIGCOMM 2001: Proceedings of the 2001 conference on Applications, technologies, architectures, and protocols for computer communications, pp. 149–160. ACM Press, New York (2001)

5. Carter, R.L., Crovella, M.E.: Server selection using dynamic path characterization in wide-area networks. In: INFOCOM 1997: Proceedings of the Sixteenth Annual Joint Conference of the IEEE Computer and Communications Societies. Driving the Information Revolution, 1014 (1997)
6. Heckmann, O., Bock, A.: The edonkey 2000 protocol. Technical Report KOM Technical Report 08/2002, Darmstadt University of Technology (2002)
7. Skevik, K.A., Goebel, V., Plagemann, T.: Design, prototype and evaluation of a network monitoring library. In: Rong, C., Jaatun, M.G., Sandnes, F.E., Yang, L.T., Ma, J. (eds.) ATC 2008. LNCS, vol. 5060. Springer, Heidelberg (to appear, 2008)

A Framework for In-Network Management in Heterogeneous Future Communication Networks

Christopher Foley[1], Sasitharan Balasubramaniam[1], Eamonn Power[1],
Miguel Ponce de Leon[1], Dmitri Botvich[1],
Dominique Dudkowski[2], Giorgio Nunzi[2], and Chiara Mingardi[2]

[1] Telecommunications Software & Systems Group – Waterford Institute of Technology
Waterford, Ireland
{ccfoley,sasib,epower,miguelpdl,dbotvich}@tssg.org
[2] NEC Laboratories Europe, Network Research Division, Heidelberg, Germany
{dominique.dudkowski,giorgio.nunzi,chiara.mingardi}@nw.neclab.eu

Abstract. Future communication networks will be composed of a diversity of highly heterogeneous network variants, ranging from energy constrained wireless sensor networks to large-scale wide area networks. The fact that the size and complexity of such networks will experience tremendous growth will eventually render existing traditional network management paradigms unfeasible. We propose the radically new paradigm of *in-network management,* which targets the embedding of self-management capabilities deep inside the network nodes. In this paper, we focus on our *framework for in-network management,* which allows management logic to be embedded and executed within network nodes. Based on a specific use-case of bio-inspired network management, we demonstrate how our framework can be exploited in a network failure scenario using quorum sensing and chemotaxis.

Keywords: in-network management, bio-inspired self-management.

1 Introduction

A new management paradigm for the Future Internet is being developed within the 4WARD project, driven by a European consortium under the FP7 research program. The proposed "In-Network Management" (INM) paradigm leverages on the high integration of management functions with the network components: management functions are seen as embedded capabilities, which differ radically from the traditional design and deployment of management functions as add-on features. The benefits range from increased network autonomicity to reduced cost of integration.

While embedding management capabilities in the network itself is a promising approach, this level of integration requires well defined functions in the network element: the question addressed by this paper is whether the INM paradigm can be deployed maintaining a certain level of generality and extensibility, which are two necessary properties of complex management systems.

INM does not bring incremental improvements to existing network functionalities like much of the autonomic community have been following. Instead, INM is

S. van der Meer, M. Burgess, and S. Denazis (Eds.): MACE 2008, LNCS 5276, pp. 14–25, 2008.

pursuing a *clean slate design* for the Future Internet in an attempt to radically redesign today's networks based on novel principles. With this respect, 4WARD follows other similar initiatives of different research communities, like [15, 16]. Nevertheless, the INM paradigm appears as a novel paradigm not covered by these initiatives.

This paper introduces our current state of a framework for INM, which follows a clean-slate design approach. It seeks to support the management tasks of the future Internet, from the deployment to the running of management functions as embedded management capabilities in the network, to their interaction and collaboration. The framework will enable network operators to have greater knowledge, make the networks easier to manage, and lessen the workload on operators to spend increased time working with the Operation and Support Systems.

Chapter 2 introduces our INM paradigm. The basic framework components are discussed in Chapter 3. In Chapter 4, we provide a detailed case study based on bio-inspired networks to show how the INM framework can be exploited. Related work is discussed in Chapter 5, before we conclude in Chapter 6.

2 The In-Network Management Paradigm

In-network management is a novel paradigm that proposes a new approach to perform management operations in future networks. We recognize that the bottleneck of traditional solutions is structural to the paradigm of traditional approaches, where management operations are normally seen as "add-on" features of network devices: first network functions are deployed in the devices, then management functions are added to perform FCAPS operations. Reduced scalability, high integration costs, lack of automation are the first main shortcomings.

The paradigm of in-network management assumes embedded management capabilities, where several autonomous components with management capabilities inside a network element allow for a flexible composition within the same or between different devices. Consequently, management operations become strongly localized and different network elements interact based on peer-to-peer techniques.

As the first design milestone, a new definition of a framework is required to support the newly designed management capabilities. While embedded management capabilities enable highly localized management functions, a framework is in fact needed to compose management functionalities and make them work on a large scale. The objectives of the INM framework will proceed in three directions: keep a low footprint of the embedded functions in the network elements, enable discovery mechanisms and support dynamic deployment of management capabilities.

The first architectural element is to which extent we can push management capabilities inside a component. For this reason, we defined different degrees of embedding, which help in guiding the definition of management functions as embedded management capabilities. The degrees are defined as follows: **Inherent** management capabilities are an integral and inseparable part of a functional component's logic which cannot be altered. **Integrated** management capabilities are internal to a functional component, but separable from a functional component's logic. They allow for

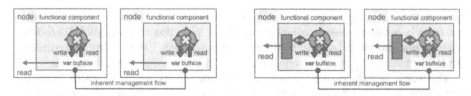

Fig. 1. Example of inherent (left) and integrated (right) management capabilities

paradigms to load management capabilities into a functional component. **External** management capabilities are located on another node.

This categorization is an instrument to deploy the INM paradigm while maintaining generality and extensibility. For example, the inherent model can be used to support protocol-specific congestion control mechanisms and to integrate them into the management plane of INM, as depicted in Fig. 1 (left). Today, TCP and SCTP have an inherent congestion control mechanism: a fault management tool requires additional read operations to monitor several counters from the nodes. We can see the difference between the traditional approach, where separated management functions must be put in place after network deployment, contrasted by the INM paradigm, which is based on a new architecture of embedded management capabilities.

The inherent model introduces a well defined interface to access the embedded capabilities. The integrated model maintains extensibility of a component's capabilities. As an example, we show in Fig. 1 (right) how this model can be used.

We believe that this categorization enables a lean and yet extensible software deployment. The next section shows how embedded capabilities can be deployed to perform more complex management operations.

3   Framework for In-Network Management

The diversity of node types which the proposed framework addresses is extensive. The design of the framework architecture must satisfy the requirements coming from both a small sensor node and also a powerful server node. Therefore it must be modular, in that the most fundamental components or artefacts can be easily exposed and also that the more high level components can be easily added and extended.

Fig. 2 shows the components which make up the framework architecture. The architecture defines a runtime environment in which functional components may be deployed. Within the runtime environment a number of levels of abstraction are defined that are relative to the amount of capabilities which a functional component makes accessible to other components and applications. The architecture also defines specific services which aid the running of functional components and applications. They are utilities within the architecture and are named InNetMgmt Services.

The InNetMgmt Kernel is a privileged area within the architecture where components or services which run here are protected from application interference, in that access to artefacts inside of the InNetMgmt Kernel is restricted. Security measures exist when accessing this area of the architecture.

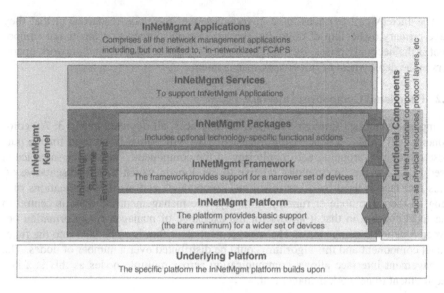

Fig. 2. High-level node architecture

3.1 Framework Components

The **InNetMgmt Runtime Environment** is a container in which functional components and, InNetMgmt Services can execute. The Runtime Environment contains three layers or levels of abstraction: the InNetMgmt Platform, the InNetMgmt Framework and the InNetMgmt Packages. These three levels are abstractions of the most fundamental libraries and capabilities to make InNetMgmt components and applications run. Additional packages are needed for more advanced functionality supported by specific device types.

Functional Components are logical entities inside a node that may contain some management capabilities or the ability to link to management capabilities in order to participate in the execution of a management function or algorithm. A functional component can be anything such as a device driver, a protocol layer, a service, or part of a service. Functional components can be dedicated management components in that their primary purpose is to execute dedicated management logic. They can also exist with just functional logic and not have any explicit management logic.

InNetMgmt Services are utilities within the framework which can take a number of forms and perform a number of functions. Their primary tasks is to provide fundamental support for InNetMgmt functionality, e.g. a command mediation service which provides a mechanism which applications can use to issue commands to and receive responses from functional components. An InNetMgmt service could be used as an alarm/event publication facility which could be availed of by applications. The developed InNetMgmt services will be relative to the capabilities of the node itself and to the features which is supported by the Runtime Execution Environment.

Another task which may be assigned to an InNetMgmt Service is the management of the functional components. This includes the starting, stopping and management of dependencies between components.

The InNetMgmt Services have governance over the node resources in that they have primary ownership of them, but this may be outsourced to a functional component if the necessity arises. InNetMgmt services assist developers and network operators in the deployment of in-network management.

3.2 Functional Component Interface Types

Components interact through a number of interfaces, all depicted in Fig 3. All components will expose a supervision interface. This will primarily be used for the purpose of starting, stopping and monitoring of the component. The service interface is used to expose the functionality relative to the domain which it is representative of. This interface is used by other functional components and also by applications running on the same node or running remotely. The management interface is central to the INM concept in that it allows for the exchange of management information between functional components. The management algorithm is embedded into the functional component and this algorithm could be distributed over a number of nodes. The management interface allows communication across multiple nodes as this is a key requirement to network management.

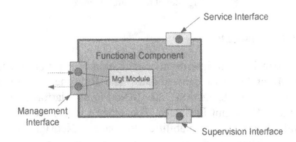

Fig. 3. Functional Component Interface Types

3.3 Management Function Calls

Whether a component or utility service resides in user or utility space depends on the functionality it contains. The fact that management logic can be running in a component in the kernel of a networked node is one of the key features of the INM paradigm. This gives the possibility to potentially analyze packets passing through the node and inject new or modified packets back onto the network. In-Network management does not just provide high abstractions from a network management level, it enables management at as low a level as possible. Because of the traversal of space, the framework will provide a bridge which will link the management of components and services across both user and kernel space.

4 Case Study

Some bio-inspired techniques applied to routing were chosen as the case study because it highlights the potential which exists by adopting the INM paradigm. The proposed framework when complete can avail of these techniques and algorithms as they can be embedded right down at a very low level within the node.

Our proposed bio-inspired techniques that have been applied to this case study are based on our biological framework for autonomic communications [11] [9]. In particular for this case study, we have employed two specific bio-inspired techniques, including: (i) Quorum Sensing, and (ii) Chemotaxis.

1. *Quorum sensing* [8] is a mechanism used by cells to coordinate in a distributed fashion to perform specific functionalities. The process mimics reaction-diffusion [1] mechanisms of cell self-organisation, whereby cells emit chemicals to the neighbouring cells. Each neighbouring cell will evaluate the chemical concentration and determine how much of its own chemical should be emitted into the environment.

2. *Chemotaxis* is a specific mechanism of mobility used by micro-organisms, which works through attraction of chemical field formed within the environment. There are two types of chemotaxis, which includes positive and negative chemotaxis. Positive chemotaxis allows the microorganism to get attracted to a food source, for example, while a negative chemotaxis pulls the micro-organism from a specific source (e.g. Poisonous source).

4.1 Mapping of Bio-inspired Techniques

In this section we will describe how the two bio-inspired mechanisms described above will map to the INM resource management process of mesh networks. Large-scale networks with a large number of nodes will require an efficient mechanism to support routing and resource management for QoS (Quality of Service), which in turn will maximise revenues of the operator. Based on our bio-inspired frameworks, the two techniques have been applied to other networking concepts; chemotaxis to routing in core wired networks [11] and quorum sensing to ad hoc social networking applications [10]. In this case study, we employ the two techniques in a similar fashion to routing in a network failure scenario. An example of each of the two mechanisms is illustrated in Fig. 4.

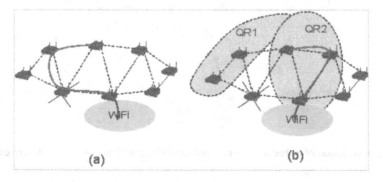

Fig. 4. Illustration of Chemotaxis (a) and Quorum Sensing (b) Techniques

The chemotaxis process allows each node to translate the resource capacity of the node in terms of gradient G_i (i – node). As the route moves from one node to the next node, the route moves along the highest gradient from source to destination. This creates a hop-by-hop route discovery effect as shown in Fig 4 (a). In the event of a node failure, the nodes will collaborate with each other to invoke traffic prioritisation (this is due to the fact that there is not enough capacity to support all diverted traffic). The collaboration will be based on the revenue objective of the operators and the dropping of certain traffic types to maintain a certain level of revenue. The negotiation process and collaboration is based on the quorum sensing mechanism. As shown in Fig 4 (b), two quorum sensing regions are formed in the network (QR1 and QR2, based on traffic capacity capability). Since QR2 provides a larger amount of capacity for the diverted traffic, the gradient is higher, leading the diverted traffic to move to QR2.

It is interesting to verify how these embedded capabilities can be actually accessed and controlled by an operator. While communication between nodes can be accomplished with peer-to-peer techniques[1], the composition of embedded capabilities and their linkage to an operator's objectives is a crucial design aspect of INM. Following the architecture principles of Fig 2, a point of attachment with the operator can be deployed as an INM application, attached to the kernel.

This application would then be responsible to retrieve the objectives and disseminate them in the network. Only one node is required to deploy this application, because each node is responsible to disseminate the behaviour inside the network in a P2P fashion. It should be noted that this is different from other approaches, where a

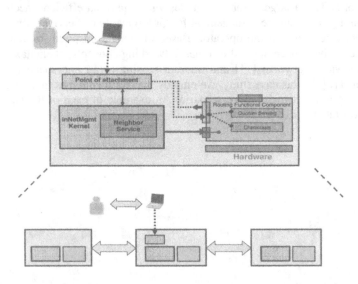

Fig. 5. Inclusion of embedded bio-inspired capabilities with an operator's objectives

---

[1] Following the INM paradigm, it is under discussion in 4WARD whether such p2p communication should occur in-band or out-band.

policy server is required to translate objectives into a set of atomic operations and enforce them to all the devices.

Fig. 5 shows additionally how the bio-inspired techniques of Chemotaxis and Quorum Sensing would be deployed within the INM framework as embedded management capabilities. The primary interface which would be used by the modules is the management interface. It is through this interface that the gradient will be diffused between nodes and also the negotiation and collaboration process which is necessary to realize both algorithms.

Since the presented use case deals only with routing objectives, an interesting aspect and open question for the future architecture is to which extent different embedded management domains can be composed together. When different use cases are deployed together, translation of the objectives for different embedded capabilities becomes more complex.

4.2 Scenario Description

For the purpose of testing the assertions related to bio-inspired mechanism, we created and carried out tests on a wireless mesh network. We considered the network performance in a scenario to manage traffic flowing over a network and we compared conventional network technologies against a bio-inspired optimization technique.

The network represents that of an operator providing services to connected clients. The client pays for a data service and value-added services from the operator such as multimedia (on-demand TV). We refer to a wireless mesh network, because this is the technology requiring advanced management capabilities in future deployments. The same considerations are also valid for fixed networks, like routing in an optical ring within a metropolitan distribution network. We assume two QoS levels: (i) Multimedia (higher revenue), (ii) Data (lower revenue).

The test bed is illustrated in the Fig. 6. Its composition is designed to demonstrate the scenario with the minimum complexity, while demonstrating steady state conditions after a fault. For this reason, while we are testing on a mesh network, the link configuration implies that node A and C must communicate via the intermediary nodes of B and D.

The Source was connected to node A, and the Destination to node C. Both data streams commenced at the Source to the Destination over the wireless network.

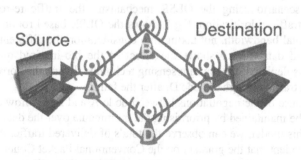

Fig. 6. Test bed setup for the reference scenario

```
*Rule*:

    {CommonName "NodeDown"}

    Events
       {Name "ConnectivityChangeEvent",
        ParameterList "NodeIdentifier", "ChangeType"}

    Conditions
       {Name "LoseNodeConnnectivity",
        If ChangeType == Disconnected}

    Actions
       {Name "ApplyTrafficWeightingForRouteCapacity",
        QueryRouteCapacity
        Params Source, Destination}
```

Fig. 7. Bio-inspired mechanism triggered through a Rule

An Optimized Link State Routing (OLSR) stack was used to configure the routes on the wireless nodes. The stack is based on the Python scripting language, which allows us to quickly embed management capabilities.

In fact, the bio-inspired fault recovery is triggered through a node down event, described in Fig. 7. This rule was implemented via the Python scripting language.

The test-case shows how a management capability can be embedded inside a node. The parameters to be configured (the TrafficWeights of Fig 8) can be accessed through the internal management interface supported by the architecture and used by any application deployed on top, like a translator of objectives.

The steps for testing each scenario are detailed below. Phase 1 represents the normal operation of the network, where traffic uses the capacity of the entire network to allow the data streams to cross, Fig. 6. In phase 2, Node D encounters a failure; therefore a portion of the traffic must be diverted to node B.

Each node's physical hardware is a Ubuntu Linux 7.10 Server-based mesh node, consisting of the following: Mini ITX PC with two Atheros-based [17] wireless network interfaces. For the OLSR testing, the Python-based pyOLSR stack was used.

4.3 Results

The results in Fig. 8 show the traffic trace that is collected at the destination. In the conventional scenario using the OLSR mechanism, the traffic re-routes with no awareness of traffic prioritisation. Fig 8 shows the OLSR-based routing traffic has a reduction of total bandwidth, not taking into consideration the different traffic types, multimedia and data. Fig. 9 shows the effect of the bio-inspired quorum sensing mechanism. As depicted, the quorum sensing technique diverts the correct proportion of multimedia traffic through to node D, after the failure

This is because of the negotiations between node A and B, to allow a certain level of revenue to be maintained by prioritising the multimedia over the data traffic.

Based on this model, we can observe the totals of delivered traffic. As is visible in Fig. 10, it is evident that the gradient on the Conventional Packet Count is not as steep as the gradient on the Bio-Inspired Packet Count. This indicates better performance by the Bio-Inspired method even after the link failure marked at time 210 on the graphs.

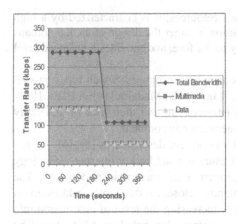

Fig. 8. Conventional Scenario

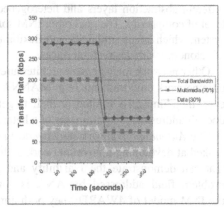

Fig. 9. Bio-Inspired Scenario

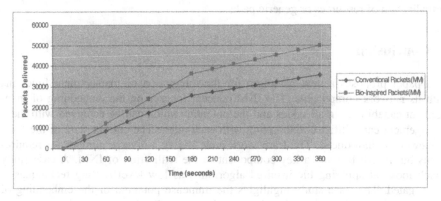

Fig. 10. Conventional Packets (Cumulative) vs. Bio-Inspired Packets (Cumulative)

5 Related Work

The authors of [6] distinguish management approaches by the *organizational model*, structured into centralized, weakly distributed and strongly distributed approaches. This model is helpful in a coarse categorization of paradigms in network management and to distinguish between traditional and more comprehensive approaches. The general trend is for network management to evolve towards strongly distributed paradigms and to provide more automation of management. However, only a few architectural and project-related solutions exist that provide a general and comprehensive approach to autonomic network management.

The FOCALE system presented in [3, 12] is characterized by a high level of autonomy, in that human interaction is only foreseen in the definition of business goals. However, the system is very complex and therefore difficult to understand in case of unforeseen failure of the management system itself. The same weakness affects the ASA architecture [13]. Although it is a generic architecture, which encompasses different abstraction layers and heterogeneous resources, it is characterized by a high level of complexity. The goal of an INM solution is rather the design of an autonomous system which keeps simplicity and flexibility to the fore, and provides a balanced level of autonomy with abstract interfaces..

Other network management architectures have been proposed, which focus on specific network environments (e.g. MANNA [7] in WSNs, Madeira [14] in P2P). However, their impact is limited to their target environment and their lack of generality doesn't address the requirements of a heterogeneous environment.

The *Autonomic Network Architecture (ANA)* project described in [5], [4], [2] has looked at developing a novel network architecture beyond legacy Internet technology that can demonstrate the feasibility and properties of autonomic networking. The problem field addressed by ANA is somehow close to the topics addressed in the INM model of 4WARD: they both aim at increasing the level of automation into the network and they follow a clean slate approach. Nevertheless ANA should be regarded as a generic architecture for autonomic devices, while INM leverages on a tight coupling of management functions with the services deployed on a device, like virtualization of resources or generic paths.

6 Conclusion

This paper proposes a new paradigm for the integration of management functions with its network components. The INM concept focuses on the embedding of management capabilities in all nodes and the potential which can be achieved with these management capabilities collaborating with each other. The current state of the INM framework is introduced. The framework must satisfy a diverse number for requirements but it will become a key component in the realisation of INM. A case study which looks at applying bio-inspired algorithms as low level routing techniques is investigated. This case study highlights the immense potential of the embedding of management capabilities at a low level in the nodes. Deployment of these management algorithms is shown with respect to the proposed framework.

Acknowledgments

The work described in this paper was partly funded by the European Union through the 4WARD project in the 7th Framework Programme Call 1.

References

1. Turing, A.M.: The Chemical basis of morphogenesis. Philosophical Transaction of the Royal Society 237, 37–72 (1952)
2. Autonomic Network Architecture (ANA). Project funded by the European Union Information Society Technologies Framework Programme 6 (EU IST FP6), http://www.ana-project.org/

3. Jennings, B., van der Meer, S., Balasubramaniam, S., Botvich, D., Foghlú, M.Ó., Donnelly, W.: Towards Autonomic Management of Communications Networks. IEEE Communications Magazine 45(10), 112–121 (2007)
4. Jelger, C., Tschudin, C., Schmid, S., Leduc, G.: Basic Abstractions for an Autonomic Network Architecture. In: Proceedings of the 1st IEEE WoWMoM Workshop on Autonomic and Opportunistic Communications (AOC 2007), Helsinki, Finland (June 2007)
5. Sestinim, F.: Situated and Autonomic Communication – an EC FET European Initiative. ACM SIGCOMM Communication Review 36(2), 17–20 (2006)
6. Martin-Flatin, J.-P., Znaty, S., Hubaux, J.-P.: A Survey of Distributed Enterprise Network and Systems Management Paradigms. Journal of Network and Systems Management 7(1), 9–26 (1999)
7. Ruiz, L.B., Nogueira, J.M., Loureiro, A.A.F.: MANNA: A Management Architecture for Wireless Sensor Networks. IEEE Communications Magazine 41(2), 116–125 (2003)
8. Miller, M.B., Bassler, B.L.: Quorum sensing in Bacteria. Annual Review in MicroBiology, 165–199 (2001)
9. Agoulmine, N., Balasubramaniam, S., Botvich, D., Strassner, J., Lehtihet, E., Donnelly, W.: Challenges for Autonomic Network Management. In: 1st Conf. on Modelling Autonomic Communication Environment (MACE), Dublin, Ireland (2006)
10. Balasubramaniam, S., Botvich, D., Gu, T., Donnelly, W.: Chemotaxis and Quorum Sensing inspired Interaction supporting Social Networking. In: Proceedings of 65th IEEE Vehicular Technology Conference (IEEE VTC Spring), Dublin, Ireland (April 2007)
11. Balasubramaniam, S., Botvich, D., Donnelly, W., Foghlú, M.Ó., Strassner, J.: Bio-inspired Framework for Autonomic Communication Systems. In: Dressler, F., Carreras, I. (eds.) Advances in Biologically Inspired Information Systems: Models, Methods, and Tools. Studies in Computational Intelligence. Springer, Heidelberg (2007)
12. van der Meer, S., Donnelly, W., Strassner, J., Jennings, B., Foghlú, M.O.: Emerging Principles of Autonomic Network Management. In: 1st IEEE Int'l Workshop on Modelling Autonomic Communications Environments, Dublin, Ireland (October 2006)
13. Cheng, Y., Farha, R., Kom, M.S., Garcia, A.-L., Hong, J.W.-K.: A Generic Architecture for Autonomic Service and Network Management. Computer Communications 29(18), 3691–3709 (2006)
14. Madeira, http://www.celtic-madeira.org/index.html
15. http://cleanslate.stanford.edu/
16. http://www.ana-project.org/
17. http://www.atheros.com/

Strategy-Trees: A Feedback Based Approach to Policy Management

Bradley Simmons and Hanan Lutfiyya

The University of Western Ontario
Department of Computer Science
London, Ontario, Canada
{bsimmons,hanan}@csd.uwo.ca

Abstract. A strategy-tree is an abstraction that encapsulates and relates multiple strategies for achieving a high level directive. Policies represent the expression of *how* a strategy is to be implemented (i.e., what
to do under a set of implicit assumptions). An architecture, based on a
strategy-tree, is presented that monitors the effectiveness of the active
policy set at achieving various directives, and is able to dynamically
change strategy (policy set membership) in response to poor performance. An initial prototype is introduced and a simulation is discussed
demonstrating the promise of this approach.

1 Introduction

A policy can be understood to represent "... any type of formal behavioural
guide" that is input to the system [1]. This implies that service level agreements
(SLAs), business objectives and business rules can all be considered as policies.
SLAs codify an agreement between a service provider and client about what
the provider is responsible to provide to the client. Business objectives can be
understood as constraints on business metrics (i.e., increase profit by five percent
per quarter). Business rules are used to guide the decision making process during
operation i.e., how to allocate resources to gold and silver service clients during
contention. Previous work showed how policies from separate sources can be
related [2].

Little work has been done on evaluating the efficacy of the policy sets being used for management. For example, a data center provider hosting multiple
application environments of various service classes may have a high level objective to increase quarterly profits by five percent. A policy that may be among
those deployed to achieve this objective is the following: *Always favor gold class
application environments when considering re-allocation of resources to clients
per management cycle.* Underlying the polices that describe how to treat various
application environments are implicit assumptions. For instance, one assumption may be about the high expected loyalty of bronze application environment
customers. However, should this assumption prove false and if gold application
environments starve out bronze application environments for extended periods

S. van der Meer, M. Burgess, and S. Denazis (Eds.): MACE 2008, LNCS 5276, pp. 26–37, 2008.

of time, a negative impact may be felt by the data center provider with regards to achieving its higher level objective.

The case of an ISP providing DiffServ to its clients is also worth considering in more detail. Assume the following policy is among those deployed: *Gold class traffic is guaranteed 15% of total bandwidth*. Underlying the policies that describe how to treat the various traffic flows (i.e., gold, silver, bronze) are implicit assumptions. For example, the ISP provider may assume that there will always be some minimum amount of gold class traffic. However, in a scenario where unexpectedly gold traffic does not exist while simultaneously an overload of bronze traffic occurs, the withholding of 15% of bandwidth for non-existent gold traffic may have a negative impact on ISP profit. Specifically, not only is the available bandwidth not being utilized but non-gold traffic will potentially experience degraded service.

To address this limitation in current approaches, strategy-trees are introduced. A strategy can be defined informally as "...a plan designed to achieve a particular long-term aim" [3]. Strategy-trees are an abstraction that encapsulates and relates multiple strategies for achieving a high level directive. Since a policy set is the expression of how a strategy is to be implemented (i.e., what to do under a set of implicit assumptions) a strategy-tree assumes that multiple policy sets have been designed for achieving a high-level objective under various sets of assumptions.

After design of the strategy-tree, and the binding of policy sets to the leaf nodes a mechanism is provided to monitor the run-time performance at various temporal granularities and to utilize this feedback of perceived achievement or lack thereof with regards to various directives, to inform decision making with regards to maintaining or switching strategies dynamically. Put another way, the efficacy of active policy sets can be monitored and evaluated at run-time and policy set membership (as it relates to an entire strategy for achieving a high level directive) can be altered dynamically as necessary in response to observed performance.

The paper is organized as follows. Section 2 introduces a scenario which is used throughout the remainder of the paper. Section 3 presents details of the formal semantics of strategy-trees. Section 4 introduces an architecture. Section 5 presents a prototype and discusses pertinent implementation details. Section 6 describes a simulation. Section 7 describes related work. Section 8 concludes with a discussion and a consideration of future work.

2   Scenario

In order to better describe strategy-trees and the usage of strategy-trees for management the following scenario is presented and referred to throughout the remainder of this paper. Consider a data center, with two registered clients, managed using the policy-based management (PBM) framework presented previously in [4,5,2]. Client applications are registered with the data center provider. An application environment is the physical set of hardware allocated to that application. Every hour, a periodic review occurs at which time the Global Perspective Manager (GPM) polls all Application Environment Managers (AEMs) about their future resource needs. Then, based on multiple policies from several sources, a global optimization model is constructed and solved defining resource allocation for the following period which are then applied to the application environments.

The first application environment (AE_1) has registered for a best-effort class of service as defined in its SLA with the provider. The second application environment (AE_2) has registered for an enhanced gold class of service as defined in its SLA with the provider. AE_1 has the following SLA details (this is a brief excerpt of several pertinent service level objectives (SLOs) from the SLA). AE_1 is in class 1 and this implies that the application environment is willing to pay one monetary unit per requested machine per management cycle for any machine provisioned to it in addition to the minimum number negotiated, tier 0 has a minimum guaranteed number of servers of 2, tier 1 has a minimum guaranteed number of servers of 3 and tier 2 has a minimum guaranteed number of servers of 3 as well. AE_2 has the following SLA details (this is a brief excerpt of several pertinent SLOs from the SLA). AE_2 is in class 0 which implies that the application environment is willing to pay two monetary unit per requested machine per management cycle for any machine provisioned to it in addition to the minimum number negotiated, tier 0 has a minimum guaranteed number of servers of 2, tier 1 has a minimum guaranteed number of servers of 4 and tier 2 has a minimum guaranteed number of servers of 4 as well.

3   Formal Semantics of a Strategy-Tree

A strategy-tree is a directed acyclic graph $ST = (V, E)$ composed of a set of vertices V and a set of edges E. Each vertex $v_i \epsilon V$ represents a node in this strategy-tree. Each edge $e_i \epsilon E$ represents a relationship between nodes. Nodes can be one of three node types: a directive type, an AND type or an OR type. Directive type nodes encapsulate a goal on achieving some value for a metric (values for multiple metrics). This metric could be as simple as a technical metric (i.e., throughput) or as complex as a business metric (i.e., increase in profit by 5% per quarter). AND type nodes aggregate a set of child nodes at a specific depth. OR type nodes are used as *choice points* within a strategy-tree allowing for the selection of only one child node out of at least two. This is discussed in more detail in Section 4.3.

All nodes have an associated quantum attribute (denoted by *node.quantum*). The quantum attribute value of a parent node should always be greater than or equal to the associated quantum attribute value of any of its direct child nodes. In practice *parent-node.quantum* modulo *child-node.quantum* should be equal to zero (the reason for this will be explained in Section 3.3). The directive type nodes have in-degree of one and out-degree of one or zero. The AND and OR type nodes have in-degrees of one and out-degrees of n such that $n \geq 2$.

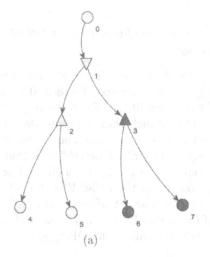

Index	Quantum Attribute Value
0	168
1	24
2	1
3	1
4	1
5	1
6	1
7	1

(a)   (b)

Fig. 1. (a) The strategy-tree defined for the case study. Two strategies are defined S_1 (0,1,2,4,5) and S_2 (0,1,3,6,7). Circles represent directive type nodes, triangles represent AND type nodes and upside down triangles represent OR type nodes. (b) A chart displaying the various quantum attribute values for the nodes indexed in the strategy-tree.

A strategy-tree must contain at least one OR type node and at least three directive type nodes (this is referred to as a minimum strategy-tree). This is necessary because one of the main purposes of a strategy-tree is to encapsulate multiple strategies and in order to have different strategies an OR type node is needed to provide alternatives. The root must be of directive type node and all leaves must be of directive type node as well. Every edge e_i in a strategy-tree is directed and connects two vertices such that a vertex v_i at depth n is connected to a vertex v_j at depth $n+1$. There are no self-loops and there are no multiple edges from any vertex v_i to any other vertex v_j. As long as the root and terminus nodes are all directive type nodes, any internal combination of nodes is acceptable.

The strategy-tree, Fig. 1(a), for managing the data center in the scenario has as its highest-level directive, node 0, which specifies the following: *In a 168 hour period daily directives should have been met greater than 50 % of the time (i.e., greater than 3/7 times)*. The four remaining directive nodes are leaf nodes and specify the following directives. Node four: *SLA minima must be met for each application environment per management cycle*. Node five: *Each management cycle, at least 50 % of all dynamically requested resources should be allocated per application environment*. Node six: *SLA minima must be maintained for each application environment per management cycle*. Node seven: *Each management cycle, at least 50 % of all dynamically requested resources should be allocated to each class 0 application environment*.

3.1 Strategy

Definition 1. *A strategy specifies one possible way of achieving the highest level directive (i.e., root node of the strategy-tree).*

The strategy-tree, Fig. 1(a), for managing the data center in the scenario is composed of two strategies. The first strategy, S_1 is composed of nodes (0,1,2,4,5). The second strategy, S_2 is composed of the nodes (0,1,3,6,7). A strategy-tree is defined as $ST = (V, E)$ where $V = A \cup O \cup D$ such that A represents the set of AND type nodes, O represents the set of OR type nodes and D represents the set of directive type nodes. A *strategy* $= (V', E')$ is defined such that the following properties hold: (i) The root node $r\epsilon V$ of the ST is an element of the strategy such that $r\epsilon V'$; (ii) A strategy consists of the nodes $V' = (A', O', D')$ such that $A' \subseteq A$, $O' \subseteq O$ and $D' \subset D$; (iii) The set of leaves $L \subset D'$ such that $\mid L \mid > 1$ and $\forall l \epsilon L$ the out-degree of $l = 0$; (iv) Every child of an AND type node $n\epsilon A$ is included in a strategy; and (v) One child of an OR type node $n\epsilon O$ is included in a strategy.

Theorem 1. *A strategy-tree has at least $n + 1$ possible strategies where n is the number of OR type nodes (An inductive proof on the number of OR type nodes in a strategy-tree is omitted due to space limitations).*

3.2 Policies

Policies are bound to the leaf nodes of the strategy-tree. The following are the policies (stated informally) under which the GPM functions when strategy S_1 is active. Policy 1. *If an application environment sends a Node Down Event (NDE) to the GPM then the GPM should replace the node immediately from the resource pool if there are enough resources available.* Policy 2. *An application environment should always have more than or equal its minimum number of servers per tier.* Policy 3. *If an application environment requests resources at a periodic review and if resources are available then fill the request.* Policy 3 is switched to 3' in the event that S_2 is the active strategy. The implication is that 3 and 3' are bound to nodes 5 and 7 respectively. Policy 3'. *Satisfy gold class application environment requests for resources before other resource requests.*

3.3 The Quantum Attribute of a Node

In order to be able to utilize strategy-trees for management purposes there are three important operations that must be facilitated: (i) It must be possible to monitor and determine whether a directive is being met; (ii) The values of lower level nodes must be able to be passed up the strategy-tree and used at a higher levels; and (iii) Informed decisions about whether to continue using a given strategy or whether to switch must be able to be specified. The node's quantum attribute value is used to specify when these operations should be performed.

The Management Time Unit (MTU) represents the finest granularity of record-keeping with regards to management function that the underlying management system is capable of recording. A node's quantum attribute value acts as an integer coefficient on this MTU value. For example, the PBM framework being used in the data center scenario has a periodic review function that occurs once every hour; therefore, the MTU value is one (i.e., representing one hour). The table presented in Fig 1(b) presents the quantum attribute values for each node in the strategy-tree presented in Fig 1(a).

Nodes two through seven have quantum attribute values of one. This implies that an evaluation must be made hourly as to whether or not each directive is being met. Node one has a quantum attribute value of 24 and so its directive's satisfaction is only checked once every 24 hours. Finally, satisfaction of node zero's directive is checked once each week.

For example, consider that Strategy S_1 is the active strategy in the data center management scenario. Every hour the directives encapsulated by both leaf nodes (nodes four and five) with quantum attribute values of one must be evaluated. Specifically, an evaluation must be made as to whether SLA minima are being met for each registered application environment (AE_1 and AE_2) and whether each application environment has received 50% of all dynamically requested servers. Since a directive is either met or not met a boolean value can be used to signify the result of evaluation of the node. As the parent node, in this case is an AND type node (node two) a boolean *and* operator is applied to the results passed up to it by nodes four and five in order to determine what value should be passed up to its parent node one.

The evaluation of the leaf node directives and the subsequent pushing up of results is repeated 23 more time at which point an evaluation as to whether the directive specified on the set of 24 hourly directives has been met is made. A decision to maintain or switch the strategy must be made as well (*choice points* are discussed in much greater detail in Section 4.3). The satisfaction of node one's directive is passed up to node zero and the strategy is either maintained or a switch to S_2 occurs. If a switch occurs then a change is made in the policy set.

4 Architecture

This section describes an architecture that utilizes feedback on the effectiveness of policy sets on achieving specific directives as defined in a strategy-tree. Monitoring the run-time effectiveness of the directives encapsulated by the nodes in the active *strategy* allows for selection of alternative paths in the tree to be made dynamically leading to automated changes in utilized policy sets (i.e., dynamic changes in strategy).

4.1 Management Database

In order to monitor higher level directives through potentially complex patterns of system attainment of various metrics (i.e., monitoring the number of gold class application environments with SLA violations while also considering the increasing trend in the number of bronze application environments being registered weekly for four weeks) a management database (MDB) must be maintained that is able to (a) collect run-time information about achievement or failures with regard to achieving various directives at some minimum temporal granularity (b) to provide data mining potential to the system in order to facilitate informed feedback decisions and strategy management during operation.

4.2   Visualizing a Strategy-Tree

A mechanism for specifying strategy-trees is necessary. While a specification language is one possible approach, the structure and relationships among the various nodes of a strategy-tree are well suited to a graphical representation. A graphical editor for describing a strategy-tree would need to represent the various node types in a simple distinguishable manner. For instance, directive type nodes might be represented as circles, AND type nodes as triangles and OR type nodes as upside down triangles. Further, it would be helpful for such an editor to highlight the current *active* strategy by coloring the nodes a different color from the rest of the hierarchy. Finally, it might prove useful to present other information about the various nodes in a table beside the graph of the strategy-tree in order to maintain an uncluttered representation of the hierarchy.

4.3   Strategy-Tree Nodes

As previously discussed in Section 3 there are three types of nodes in a strategy-tree. Leaf nodes must have a mechanism for passing directives to the underlying policy based management (PBM) system (i.e., adding / removing constraints from a global optimization model). Further, all nodes must maintain a *results* list to be able to keep track of the satisfaction of their child nodes. Recall, that a boolean result is passed up from a node to it's parent each time the logic encapsulated by the node is evaluated. Also, every node must have a boolean variable *active* which is set to true when the current node is a member of the active strategy and set to false when it is not.

A SAT-element is an administrator defined mechanism for evaluating whether or not a directive, as encapsulated by a node, is being met. This is achieved in multiple ways: for directive type nodes, logic can be specified that includes querying (and in more advanced cases mining) the MDB in order to determine the success or failure of achieving the encapsulated directive. For OR type nodes an examination of the *results* list may be used in combination with queries to the MDB. While in the case of an AND type node, the result of the application of a boolean *and* operation to the values maintained in the node's *results* list (i.e., results of its child nodes) is all that is required.

A DEC-element is an administrator defined mechanism for evaluating whether to maintain or switch the current strategy and, if a change is needed, to which strategy this switch should be made. It should be pointed out that a switch in strategy refers only to the portion of a strategy below the current OR type node in the strategy-tree. DEC-elements are only associated with OR type nodes.

OR type nodes act as *choice points* (a similar idea is presented in [6] which refers to variation points) as they denote a locus for choice between separate strategies in a strategy-tree. A DEC-element should determine whether or not to switch strategies based on the current strategy which is demarcated by the *active* child of the current node, information obtained through queries of the MDB and possibly the current node's *results* list.

It is important to point out that changing strategy is more complicated than simply choosing a different child node. Specifically, the paths between a given node and leaf nodes may include OR type nodes. This implies that the administrator needs to design the selected strategy with care.

Node one, from Fig 1(a), is the only *choice point* in the strategy-tree presented for the data center management scenario; therefore, it has both a SAT-element and a DEC-element defined for it. The SAT-element for this node simply examines its *results* list and if less than 13 of the 24 entries are true it returns false otherwise it returns true. While this SAT-element is similar to the other previously defined SAT-elements, the DEC-element is not. Specifically, *choice points* provide a locus for expert decision making code to be run. The following sections describes two possible alternative versions of the DEC-element defined for node one. Both following sections refer to Fig. 1(a), 1(b) when referring to indexes.

Basic Approach. If the current active strategy is S_1 and the SAT-element for node one returned false, implying that greater than 50% of the current node's *results* list elements are false then the current strategy should be switched to S_2. However, if the SAT-element returned true, then the strategy should be left unchanged. Conversely, if the current active strategy is S_2 and the SAT-element for node one returned false, implying that greater than 50 % of the current node's *results* list elements are false, then there is no reason to consider switching back as this strategy is much more greedy already. However, if the SAT-element returned true it is time to switch back to S_1.

Refined Approach. This second example considers a more nuanced approach. If the current strategy is S_1 and the SAT-element for node one returned false, implying that greater than 50% of the current node's *results* list elements are false before switching to the alternative strategy, this DEC-element would examine the previous epoch (i.e., the set of MTU increments since its last evaluation) to determine if there had been a sequence of five or more failures to any class 0 application environments. This added check is based on the premise that if only class 1 application environments are suffering degraded service then there is no reason to switch to one that favors class 0 application environments. However, if this is found to be the case then a switch to strategy S_2 is performed. In the event that the SAT-element returned true then no change is required and so the current strategy is maintained.

If the current strategy is S_2 and the SAT-element for node one returned false, implying that greater than 50% of the current node's (i.e., node one's) *results* list elements are false, then the current strategy has not improved performance;

however, since no benefit will be gained through switching back to the best-effort approach the current strategy is maintained and it will be left up to a higher *choice point* (i.e., not presented in this paper) to change the current approach upon its evaluation later. If the the SAT-element returned true, before switching back to the S_1 strategy this DEC-element ensures that there have been no failures to class 0 environments in the preceding epoch. If this is the case, then a switch to the alternative strategy is performed, otherwise, switching is deemed to risky and the current strategy is maintained.

4.4   Algorithm

The architecture at present is composed of several individual pieces. The interaction of the pieces is encapsulated in and coordinated by the *evaluateCurrentStrategy* algorithm that is described in this section. It is intended that this algorithm will be called by the underlying management system each time the MTU is incremented. For the data center management scenario, the GPM would call this algorithm at the completion of each periodic review.

The algorithm *evaluateCurrentStrategy*, is presented in Fig. 2. When the algorithm is executed, all nodes in the currently *active* strategy are examined, from leaves to root (hence the call to buildActiveList on line 2 in the algorithm) and when the currentMTUIncrement value (passed in to the algorithm) modulo the current node's quantum attribute value is equal to zero, the node's associated SAT-element is executed.

The *execSAT* algorithm, which is called on line 6, is used to encapsulate the execution of a node's SAT-element. For the AND type nodes this simply involves applying a boolean *and* operation to the values of the node's *results* list (this results in a boolean result of true or false). Otherwise, an evaluation is made as

```
1: procedure EVALUATECURRENTSTRATEGY(strategy-tree,currentMTUIncrement)
2:     active[] ← buildActiveList(strategy-tree)
3:     names[]
4:     for all nodes n ∈ active[] do
5:         if currentMTUIncrement mod n.getQuanum() = 0 then
6:             boolean b ← execSAT(n)
7:             n.addToParentsResultsList(b)
8:             if n.type = OR then
9:                 names ← execDEC(n)
10:                strategy-tree.switchStrategy(names, n)
11:            end if
12:            n.clearResultsList()
13:        end if
14:    end for
15:    return
16: end procedure
```

Fig. 2. *Evaluatecurrentstrategy* is the main control loop algorithm that is called each MTU increment (i.e., by a management cycle) by the underlying management system

to whether or not this encapsulated directive is being achieved (resulting in a boolean result). For an OR type node this is also done; however, as it is a *choice point* the logic is concerned with determining whether or not performance is as expected. Regardless of the type of node, the result of the call to *execSAT* is then passed up to the parent of the current node, line 7. Next, if the current node is an OR type node then a call to *execDEC* is invoked.

The *execDEC* algorithm encapsulates all decision making with regards to modifying strategies. Inside this algorithm, the DEC-element of the node is executed. What is returned from execDEC is a list of names that identify any *choice point* (including the current node) and the name of the direct child to include in the current *active* strategy. The logic for determining why one choice is taken over another is unique to each environment and situation and a thorough analysis and understanding of any environment should underpin this decision making and be based on experience and experimentation. Changes in strategy imply changes in the policy set being used.

5   Prototype Implementation Details

The strategy-tree graphical editor prototype is written in Java and utilizes graphing capabilities provided by the JUNG [7] library. SAT/DEC-elements are assumed to be created as java classes and placed in the PATH of the running system in the directory *satdecclasses*. SAT and DEC-element classes are run through use of reflection in Java (instantiation is performed based on naming conventions for the classes).

The database used to implement the MDB is Derby. A package was defined called mdb that provides a simplified set of methods to facilitate querying and writing to the MDB. Currently only the GPM writes to the MDB while SAT and DEC-elements read from it to inform their function.

6   Simulation

A simulation, based on the scenario presented in Section 2 and referred to throughout the previous sections, was run using the strategy-tree presented in Figs. 1(a) and 1(b). All SAT-elements and DEC-elements were implemented as Java classes and stored in the correct directory. A set of entries was written to the MDB in order to test the functional aspects of the prototype. These entries included resource requests that would lead to contention and eventual SLA violations so that the evaluation of the strategy S_1 would fail after 24 iterations. The *evaluateCurrentStrategy* algorithm switched to S_2 from S_1 in response to this scenario as expected.

7   Related Work

Much work has been done on policy refinement and policy hierarchies [8,9, 10,11,12]. While these concepts are related to this work, they are orthogonal.

Specifically, strategy-trees are not concerned with how the policy sets are derived or with whether they are complete and conflict free. Rather, what is considered is whether the set of policies being used to manage a system is working effectively and if not, how to adjust the strategy (and thereby the set of policies) dynamically at run-time.

Goal-Oriented requirements engineering techniques have been applied by [6] to facilitate the semi-automation of high-variability business process configuration. Different business process configurations are generated based on degrees of satisfying soft goals and the relative rankings assigned to these goals by stakeholders. This work is focused at a high level of abstraction, ignores policy considerations, and is less dynamic and flexible than the strategy-tree approach.

8   Discussion and Future Work

Strategy-trees present a feedback based approach to management that is conceptually related to the MAPE-k approach of [13]. The architecture, presented in Section 4, monitors the effectiveness of policy sets to achieve various directives, through the use of SAT-elements over multiple time-scales, and facilitates the dynamic modification of policy set membership, through execution of DEC-elements at *choice points* in the strategy-tree. A prototype was described, Section 5, that allows for the graphical design of the strategy-tree and an implementation of the algorithm, *evaluateCurrentStrategy* was demonstrated to function correctly in a simulation presented in Section 6.

While much remains to be done, particularly on the validation front, the initial results have been encouraging. Our next steps will involve plugging this prototype into our PBM architecture [4,5,2] and affecting changes on the policies actually being used by the optimization model builder and solver module in the GPM (based on changes to strategies).

The prototype currently requires an administrator to create the SAT and DEC-element classes from scratch; likely this will be at least semi-automated in the future (i.e., automatically generated stubs).

Extension to the MDB functionality will also be explored. Specifically, while we are applying a degree of temporal reasoning onto our evaluations through use of a *results* list, actual machine learning techniques might prove interesting to explore for longer term strategic decisions and for making more nuanced decisions in various DEC-elements (i.e., at *choice points*).

Another point that has come to our attention as we developed the strategy-tree approach involves the potential utility of constraints on the structure of a strategy-trees. For example, consider whether it makes sense to allow an OR type node to have as its parent a directive type node which both share the same node quantum attribute value. Presently, we leave it unconstrained; however, this requires more thought and will be explored in the future.

Separating the logic, at OR type nodes, into SAT-elements and DEC-elements was intentional. The reasoning that led to this choice is as follows. Whether a strategy is working is a decision that has no bearing on whether or not the current *active* strategy is to be maintained. Specifically, the determination of success or failure is informational only to the parent of this node while a change in strategy is only relevant to the descendants of the current node.

Acknowledgements

Thanks to IBM Centre for Advanced Studies (CAS) in Toronto and the Natural Sciences and Engineering Research Council (NSERC) of Canada for their support.

References

1. Kephart, J., Walsh, W.: An Artificial Intelligence Perspective on Autonomic Computing Policies. In: POLICY 2004: Proceedings of the Fifth IEEE International Workshop on Policies for Distributed Systems and Networks. IEEE Computer Society, Washington (2004)
2. McCloskey, A., Simmons, B., Lutfiyya, H.: Policy-Based Dynamic Provisioning in Data Centers Based on SLAs, Business Rules and Business Objectives. In: Network Operations and Management Symposium, 2008. NOMS 2008. 11th IEEE/IFIP, pp. 1–4 (2008)
3. AskOxford.com, http://www.askoxford.com/concise_oed/strategy
4. Simmons, B., Lutfiyya, H., Avram, M., Chen, P.: A Policy-Based Framework for Managing Data Centers. In: Network Operations and Management Symposium, 2006. NOMS 2006. 10th IEEE/IFIP, pp. 1–4 (2006)
5. Simmons, B., McCloskey, A., Lutfiyya, H.: Dynamic Provisioning of Resources in Data Centers. In: ICAS 2007: Proceedings of the Third International Conference on Autonomic and Autonomous Systems. IEEE Computer Society, Washington (2007)
6. Lapouchnian, A., Yu, Y., Mylopoulos, J.: Requirements-Driven Design and Configuration Management of Business Processes. In: Alonso, G., Dadam, P., Rosemann, M. (eds.) BPM 2007. LNCS, vol. 4714, pp. 246–261. Springer, Heidelberg (2007)
7. JUNG, http://jung.sourceforge.net/doc/index.html
8. Moffett, J.D., Sloman, M.S.: Policy Hierarchies for Distributed System Management. IEEE JSAC Special Issue on Network Management 11, 9 (1993)
9. Wies, R.: Using a Classification of Management Policies for Policy Specification and Policy Transformation. In: Proceedings of the fourth international symposium on Integrated network management IV, pp. 44–56. Chapman & Hall Ltd, London (1995)
10. Mont, M., Baldwin, A., Goh, C.: POWER Prototype: Towards Integrated Policy-Based Management. In: Network Operations and Management Symposium, 2000, NOMS 2000. IEEE/IFIP, pp. 789–802 (2000)
11. Bandara, A.K., Lupu, E.C., Moffett, J., Russo, A.: A Goal-based Approach to Policy Refinement. In: POLICY 2004: Proceedings of the Fifth IEEE International Workshop on Policies for Distributed Systems and Networks. IEEE Computer Society, Washington (2004)
12. Rubio-Loyola, J., Serrat, J., Charalambides, M., Flegkas, P., Pavlou, G.: A Functional Solution for Goal-Oriented Policy Refinement. In: POLICY 2006: Proceedings of the Seventh IEEE International Workshop on Policies for Distributed Systems and Networks, pp. 133–144. IEEE Computer Society, Washington (2006)
13. An architectural blueprint for autonomic computing. IBM (2004)

Goal-Oriented Autonomic Process Modeling and Execution for Next Generation Networks

Monique Calisti and Dominic Greenwood

Whitestein Technologies AG
Pestalozzistrasse 45, 8044, Switzerland
http://www.whitestein.com

Abstract. The effective modeling, execution and maintenance of business and operations processes, such as those described by the eTOM process framework, is of utmost importance to Telecom organizations, especially those transitioning toward NGN infrastructure. Many Business Process Management Systems, BPMS, available today however are significantly restricted in their support for intuitive and expressive process models, run-time process agility and rapid process adaptation to cope with changing business and operational conditions. This paper discusses a means of mitigating these limitations with a highly expressive goal-oriented process management language, GO-BPMN, and innovative autonomic BPMS called LS/ABPM. Together, GO-BPMN and LS/ABPM offer an intuitive, business-driven path to creating directly executable goal-oriented process models whose structure encodes multiple degrees of freedom through the potential for late decision-making. Executing models can be structurally modified in real-time in response to autonomic feedback from underlying systems they are managing.

Keywords: business process management, next generation networks, autonomic goal-driven process navigation, service provisioning, eTOM.

1 Introduction

The implicit objective of Next Generation Networks, NGN, is to facilitate the provisioning of rich media services to the telecoms customer with short lead times and at low cost to both provider and consumer. Indeed, the widespread proliferation of low-cost bandwidth and equipment is now readily facilitating the entry of many new service providers the majority of which need to provision their services through established operator infrastructure. This naturally presents huge business potential, but only if operations can be handled effectively, i.e., safely and flexibly, at the business process level [1].

In this perspective, business and operations processes, such as those specified by the eTOM framework [2], describe how telecommunications operators and service providers should perform their daily business to, amongst other things, ensure business continuity, consistency and business-level interoperability. These processes are typically put into practice using Business Process Management

S. van der Meer, M. Burgess, and S. Denazis (Eds.): MACE 2008, LNCS 5276, pp. 38–49, 2008.

Systems, BPMS, which realize and administer a set of often diverse business processes involving people, organizations and technologies.

The major problem is that most contemporary BPMS solutions rely on well-understood, but inherently static and visually anaemic approaches to process modeling and execution. These approaches are often significantly inadequate when addressing the intrinsic flexibility and responsiveness to change required by many business processes like for instance service activation, service change management, new product assembly, procurement and supplier integration.

In particular, many of these processes face a significant level of run-time uncertainty and require process flexibility to cope effectively with changing business requirements and conditions. The primary reason for this is that most process models must be defined at design-time, rather than determined in real-time, i.e., at run-time. This implies that they can become *bloated* through the necessity of coding-in all possible options at design time due to the inability to change dynamically once in execution, *convoluted* through variation in the complexity and unpredictability of process structure, and *brittle* through an inability to adapt to real-time changes in business or operational deployment-specific conditions.

In response we propose an innovative *agile business process navigation approach* employing goal-oriented autonomic process management [3]. The approach targets the known limitations of contemporary BPMS by producing directly executable goal-oriented process models whose structures encode multiple degrees of freedom for late decision-making. The goal-oriented formalism creates a clean separation between statements of desired system behaviour, and the potential means to achieve that behaviour, encoded as plans. This approach is directly related to policy-based management of telecoms systems in that policies can both constrain decision points leading to goal satisfaction and/or be enacted through a process task taken toward achieving a goal [4]. In the former respect, predefined policies are used to control process execution by acting as conventions expressing constraints on goal directed decision points in the process model. In the latter respect, tasks can be linked to policy engines inducing a particular policy to become active in accordance with process expectations. Although not within the scope of this paper, we are currently investigating the integration of our approach to goal-oriented BPM with autonomic policy based network management [5].

Thus autonomic goal orientation offers a transition from design-time defined processes to real-time determined processes. The **Goal Orientation** aspect offers a powerful, visually intuitive method of modeling and executing processes accessible to business managers and process analysts alike. Processes are described as goal hierarchies, with every leaf goal linked to one or more plans describing that part of the overall process to be executed in order to achieve the goal. Because plans can be selected at run-time, flexibility is built-in to the process structures allowing workflows to be altered safely in real-time without any need for halting or re-starting the overall process. Moreover, **Autonomic BPM** builds on goal orientation to offer process responsiveness to change by creating feedback loops not only between the process engineer and the process model, but also between the underlying systems (human or computational) affected by the process tasks. This allows executing goal-oriented process structures to be structurally adapted in real-time in response to autonomic feedback from the underlying systems they are managing.

The remainder of this paper is organized as follows. Section 2 describes the essential principles of our goal-oriented autonomic process modeling and execution approach. The Living Systems Autonomic Business Process Management Suite, LS/ABPM, which realizes this approach, is then presented and an overview of its core components is given in Section 3. By focusing on a typical NGN composite service provisioning use case, a concrete case model is then proposed in Section 4. This aims to show how GO-BPMN can be adopted in the NGN context as a powerful and intuitive notation for business processes modeling and execution to empower business decision makers and IT administrators at different levels. On the other hand, this hopes to stimulate discussion, as summarized in Section 5, about which specific business process modeling and execution aspects might need to be further developed/refined to properly address the specific needs of increasingly dynamic NGN.

2   Goal Oriented Autonomic Process Management

In day-to-day business operations, it is quite natural to set goals, decompose a goal into sub-goals, define or reuse plans, and routinely track and check the execution of chosen plans in order to detect problems as they occur (or even better before they do), and to take appropriate actions [6].

On the other hand, todays dominant process management approaches focus almost exclusively on procedures. The concept of what the procedure is meant to achieve, and why, typically remains implicit in the mind of the humans who designed it. Because of this, the increase in process management automation that occurred with the increasing availability of BPM systems has also shifted the focus away from goals and plans in favour of procedures.

The consequence is that processes have become more efficient in execution but more rigid in structure. To support efficiency without sacrificing agility we propose that goal-orientation be placed at center stage.

2.1   Goals and Plans

Using a goal-oriented approach separates the statement of desired system behaviour, from the possible ways to perform that behaviour. A desired result is described by achievement conditions to make true and as maintenance invariants whose violation must be avoided: achieve goals and maintain goals, respectively.

The possible ways to obtain a result are represented by plans. These are essentially process graphs decorated with the conditions under which they become applicable and the results they obtain when successful.

Plans consist of a structured aggregation of tasks connected with standard Business Process Modeling Notation (BPMN) flow logic [8]. The tasks are contained within a plan body, which has a context condition describing when that body can be executed.

We developed a specific extension to the widely used BPMN visual modeling language, called GO-BPMN, or Goal Oriented BPMN [3]. The language introduces new model elements for goals, plans, relationships between them, and context variables for process-wide state preservation.

In accordance with GO-BPMN, a **goal** is an objective function that becomes active whenever its specified preconditions are met. Once any plan associated with a goal complete, the goal is considered to be satisfied. GO-BPMN specifies the following two goal types:

- *Achievement Goals* represent a condition or a state of a process that is to be achieved. These goals can thus be used to represent explicit objectives, needs, desires, etc. achieved during process execution. An Achievement Goal can be characterized by one or more pre-conditions that must hold before the goal can complete, i.e., its sub-goals or plans are committed to. Moreover, such goals can have skip conditions where, if true, the goal is considered as achieved. Figure 1 illustrates the GO-BPMN model notation for an achievement goal using in its decoration graphical form.
- *Maintenance Goals* represent a process state that is to be maintained true. These goals can thus be used to represent explicit invariants in process execution. A Maintenance Goal is characterized by a maintain-condition that must hold during the life-time of the goal. If the maintain-condition is false, any sub-goals or plans are committed to. Figure 2 illustrates the GO-BPMN model notation for a maintenance goal.

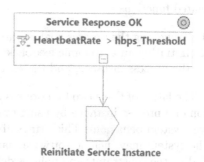

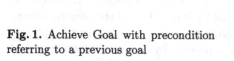

Fig. 1. Achieve Goal with precondition referring to a previous goal

Fig. 2. Maintain Goal with plan to be executed if guard conditions are false

Goals can be decomposed into *hierarchies* as shown in Figure 4. In this example the top-level goal can only complete once all three sub-goals have completed. Note that sub-goals may not need to complete successfully if the precondition on the top-level goal allows for this. All three sub-goals may execute concurrently.

A **plan** is that part of a process which specifies the functional tasks to be performed to achieve goals. Typically plans can be expressed in the form of a

BPMN model and characterized by a guard-condition that must hold before the plan can be executed. Guard conditions can incorporate the expression of context associated with the systems affected by the plan structure resulting in context-aware plan selection and execution.

As illustrated in Figure 3, multiple plans can be available to satisfy any given leaf goal at run-time. Dynamic plan selection is performed by evaluating plan guard conditions against the current process context described by the collection of goals that are presently in an active state. Selected plans are immediately executed. Additional policies can be specified to select between plans when more than one has true guard conditions.

Fig. 3. Situation where two plans are available to a goal condition

2.2   Autonomic Process Control

Once a process model has been created it can be directly executed as a process instance by associating it with an autonomous process controller that then becomes responsible for the instances entire execution. This consists of two major related functions:

1. Triggering the process goal hierarchy and controlling its run-time execution.
2. Initiating an autonomic feedback loop between the system being affected by the process instance, and the executing process instance model itself.

The latter of these two functions is responsible for initiating real-time adaptation of a process instance by using event triggers and, if desired, logic reasoning over system behaviour. This brings about both process flexibility and resilience. The system may include software, hardware, human and physical resources including the constraints and policies defining their use. Two of the possible effects of this adaptation are dynamic goal decomposition and dynamic optimization.

A process controller can self-optimise a process by assessing whether a goal hierarchy can be partially fragmented into sub-goals to parallelize execution or achieve partial results. This is particularly useful when a goal cannot be achieved due to non-satisfiable precondition and where segmenting the goal into sub-goals will allow at least some proportion of the goal condition to be met. Also, temporal pre-conditions can be adapted to alter the order of goal succession when possible and appropriate. Thus, the autonomic feedback loop is used to sense when goal hierarchies can be reformulated according to strategic beliefs held by the autonomous controller, and then acting to restructure the process as appropriate. An example of how this might restructure a process instance model is shown in Figure 4, where the 'Service Deployment Verified goal has been fragmented into three sub-goals that are performed concurrently.

A process controller can also self-optimize a process by assessing whether an existing plan can, or should, be structurally altered (re-constituting the task steps), removed entirely or have its preconditions modified. Equally, a new plan may be introduced in real-time. New plans may be discovered from plan repositories or constructed on-the-fly. In this case the autonomic feedback loop is used to sense the basis for a decision whereby alterations in the process plan structures are made. An example of one case in which this might restructure a process instance model is shown in Figure 5, where the 'Auto-Select Responsible' plan from Figure 3 has been replaced entirely with the alternative plan - same name but different precondition.

Fig. 4. Fragmentation of a goal into three sub-goals

Fig. 5. Replacement of a plan - with reference to Figure 3

A further feature of this method of process control is that process models can be updated using a modeling tool and re-loaded into the process controller in real-time. The controller will manage dependencies and state preservation, ensuring that model execution remains uninterrupted as the adjustments are blended in non-disruptively.

Interactions between process instances are managed via communication between the process controllers responsible for those instances. This is local if the instance is managed by the same controller and remote if not. Interactions can be simple bindings between the goals and plans of different processes or more complex (potentially semantic) relationships coordinating the activities of more that one controller. When multiple process instances are interacting, the influence from autonomic feedback loops is carefully monitored and controlled to ensure all effects are traceably causal and without unexpected side-effects.

3   The LS/ABPM Suite

The GO-BPMN approach is at the core of the Living Systems Autonomic Business Process Management Suite, LS/ABPM. The business goals to be achieved are defined in the process model, providing business-oriented modeling. This goal-based process model is directly executed in the run-time environment, striving to achieve the goals by navigating the goal hierarchy. LS/ABPM is particularly well suited to businesses where processes are required to swiftly adapt to change and where the processes do not, or cannot, simply follow a strict, predefined sequence. LS/ABPM is built using the Living Systems Technology Suite [7], LS/TS, middleware and it includes the following main components:

- **Process Modeler.** The core idea behind this component is to offer an intuitive, easy to-understand and use set of tools and methodologies that both business and IT users can deploy to design, test and validate GO-BPMN business processes.

  With the LS/ABPM Modeler, see Figure 6, the end user can define goals' and plans' hierarchies, application-specific business data, functions, tasks, context conditions, and implement plans with standard BPMN elements.

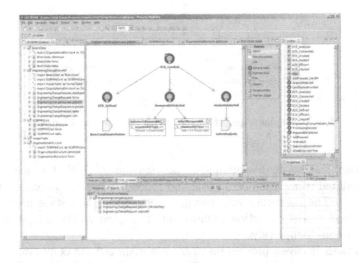

Fig. 6. The LS/ABPM Process Modeler supports GO-BPMN based design, test and validation of business processes

Moreover, this component allows the definition of organizational structures enabling the mapping of human activities to specific users, roles and organizational units.

In addition, process models are modular, allowing collaboration on large models, domain-specific modules, or libraries. In this way, different people can work on each reusable module and later consolidate their results into a whole model.

- *Process Navigation Engine.* The core idea is that GO-BPMN process models created with the Process Modeler (see above) are directly executable by the Process Navigation Engine. This component is responsible for assembling at run-time the actual business process, by creating a path that takes into account model changes and plans alternative.

According to given business goals/rules and other relevant context conditions, the Process Navigation Engine selects and orchestrate the appropriate plans in real-time. In particular, sanity conditions can be defined and the system ensures them through continuous monitoring and triggers corrective action as appropriate.

The LS/ABPM Engine implements a data-type driven Web renderer used for human-centered activities. Such a render can be customized to implement application specific front-ends.

Moreover, active coordination and cooperation between multiple process models can be achieved through message-driven synchronization between process controllers. This is an essential feature that enables to autonomically resolve competing goals and plans.

- *Management Console.* This component provides powerful tools for the deployment, management and control of processes and other system administration tasks.

First of all, continuous visibility of process execution and events is realized through detailed monitoring of running process instances, as displayed in Figure 7. At any point, the achieved, running, and waiting goals of a process can be inspected, as well as the corresponding pending tasks. This can be used by supervisors to fine-tune a process during execution.

The LS/ABPM Management Console also supports crucial control tasks such as activation/de-activation of business goals and fine-tuning of context variable governing running process instances.

Moreover, this component supports typical administrative activities such as data persistency, user management, role-based assignment of personnel, and security features.

- *Application Frameworks & Process Component Libraries.* LS/ABPM has been built as a domain independent system. However, domain-specific BPM solutions can be built by making use of the LS/ABPM SDK.

This package enables the development of system specific sets of task libraries (either human or system executable), functions, and user interface front-ends. These latter ones can also be easily enhanced or substituted by other technologies (e.g., Web frameworks) according to the specific needs.

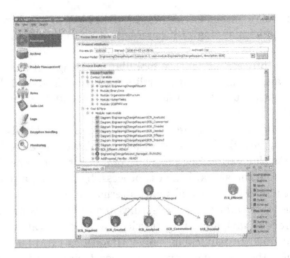

Fig. 7. The LS/ABPM Management Console showing a running process

4   Case Model: Composite Audio-Video Feed Service

This case study describes the process for creating a notional NGN composite service which provisions an audio-video feed created in real-time by combining media streams from several service sources. This Composite Audio-Video Feed, CAVF, service process is considered to be a type of telecommunications Business Service Provisioning (BSP) which typifies the envisioned form of NGN services that are statically or dynamically assembled from multiple services potentially served by multiple providers. BSP is a critical process for telecommunications operators, service providers and systems vendors as it is central to the vision of NGN. BSP, in one form or another, is addressed by both the TMF eTOM and ITIL v3 specifications.

A concrete example of the CAVF service in use is when a service provider wishes to create an audio-video (AV) feed which dynamically splices feeds from several sources to create a interleaved AV stream. The primary feed will be, for example, a television show or movie, with advertising feeds spliced into the primary feed in accordance with the target audience.

The CAVF service process has been selected as an example case due to it lending itself particularly well to process expression in terms of business goals. However, any other process defined by eTOM, ITIL, or other ad-hoc processes can be mapped into GO-BPMN and executed using the LS/ABPM navigation engine. In all cases investigated to date our approach offers clear advantages whether in terms of modeling clarity, model flexibility, sensitivity to business conditions, integration of multiple vendors, or a combination thereof.

The GO-BPMN model for provisioning the CAVF service is shown in Figure 8. The illustration shows only the goal-hierarchy, omitting all plans but three for the purposes of visual clarity. In complete models, each leaf goal must have at least one plan available for execution to be a valid model. The overall CAVF service provisioning goal, *Composite AV-Feed Service (CFS) Provisioned* is satisfied only when the five goals specified at the next, sub-layer are achieved (or de-activated, if allowed with the context of the model), and so on. The default condition is that all active goals may be achieved concurrently unless restricted by dependencies imposed by context variables specified in goal pre-conditions.

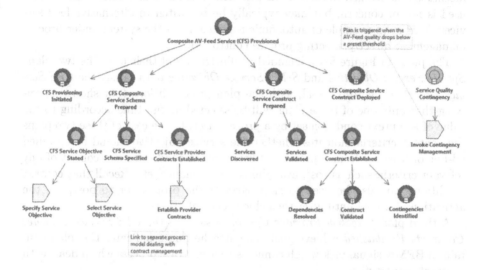

Fig. 8. GO-BPMN model for the provisioning of Composite Audio-Video Feed Service

In this particular example the second sub-layer goals are:

CFS Provisioning Initiated: Achieved when process is setup.

CFS Composite Service Schema Prepared: Achieved when the schema detailing the objective and structure of the service construct is established, and contracts established with the various providers of specified services. Although not visible in this simplified iconic notation there are logical dependencies between the three sub-goals such that *CFS Service Provider Contracts Established* can only become active once *CFS Service Schema Specified* has been achieved, which in turn can only become active once *CFS Service Objective Identified* is achieved.

CFS Composite Service Construct Prepared: Achieved when required services have been discovered and validated, and the assembled service construct is established according to the three indicated third layer sub-goals which specify that service inter-dependencies must be resolved, the entire construct must be validated and contingencies identified for cases when, for example, a service fails or a service provider violates an agreed contract.

CFS Composite Service Construct Deployed: Achieved when the service construct is successfully deployed.

Service Failure Contingency: This is a Maintain Goal which persistently monitors the quality of the AV-Feed. If the quality, measured as a function of uptime and image quality, drops below a preset threshold a contingency management mechanism is invoked to correct the problem. The particular correction method used is not of concern, but may typically be to switch to alternative feed services. This is an example of autonomic feedback from the system under process management directly affecting process control flow.

The plans in Figure 8 are included as illustration of their use. The two plans *Specify Service Objective* and *Select Service Objective* both satisfy the *CFS Service Objective Identified* goal, with the plan pre-conditions (not shown) specifying that only one of these plans will be selected at run-time according to the value of a context condition set by a process user. In the case of these two plans the context criteria indicates whether the service objective should be specified ad-hoc or selected from a prescribed list; context conditions can consist of any relevant criteria such as cost, availability, performance, etc. Recall that context conditions can also be used to skip parts of the process, or to postpone the activation of a goal until after the achievement of others.

A third plan *Establish Provider Contracts* satisfies the *CFS Service Provider Contracts Established* achieve goal. The attached note indicates this plan contains a BPMN signal task which connects to a separate process which deals with contract management.

This model is intended as an example of how the CAVF service provisioning process may be modeled, at predominantly goal-level, using GO-BPMN. As with any other GO-BPMN model executed by the LS/ABPM process navigation engine, the goal-plan-task structure can be altered, re-loaded and executed at run-time, perhaps through the addition of a new plan or segmentation of a goal into two new sub-goals. In such a case, if an instance of the model is already executing its transaction-preserved state is transferred to the new instance; a set of violation rules ensure that model alterations cannot create inconsistencies with any critical execution aspects of the original instance.

5 Conclusions

The GO-BPMN approach offers a simple and intuitive method of modeling business processes by making use of concepts and artifacts that are easy-to-understand and to express directly by business managers and process analysts. Moreover, the intrinsic flexibility built-in to the process structures implies that workflows can be safely modified in real-time without any need for stopping or re-starting the overall process. Changes to any goal or plan in a GO-BPMN process model can indeed be made indipendently and do not have a ripple effect of consequences as they would have in a sequential process model. Hence, changes can be made at any time - even during execution.

While in this paper we focused on a specific case model, we argue that the combined adoption of the GO-BPMN approach and the LS/ABPM Suite has a much broader applicability and a great potential to enable the necessary BSS/OSS evolution towards the realization of the NGN vision. In particular we recognise that while valuable as standard guidelines, the prescribed process descriptions offered by frameworks such as eTOM and ITIL are frequently a poor reflection of in-use processes that rarely follow ideal cases. This strengthens the argument favouring goal orientation, which explicitly embeds sufficient process flexibility into model descriptions while ensuring that when executing they will always achieve required and expected goals.

Acknowledgments. Thanks go to the many colleagues at Whitestein Technologies involved with this work, especially Giovanni Rimassa and Roberto Ghizzioli.

References

1. Schwartz, S.: As Telco's Become Service-Centric, They Need to Think BPM. Billing and OSS World (2005)
2. Enhanced Telecom Operations Map (eTOM). ITU-T M.3050 (2004)
3. Greenwood, D., Rimassa, G.: Autonomic Goal-Oriented Business Process Management. In: Proc. 3rd International Conference on Autonomic and Autonomous Systems, Greece (2007)
4. Raymer, D., Strassner, J., Lehtihet, E., van der Meer, S.: End-to-End Model Driven Policy Based Network Management. In: Proc. 7th IEEE International Workshop on Policies for Distributed Systems and Networks, USA (2006)
5. Bahati, R.M., Bauer, M.A., Vieira, E.M., Baek, O.K., Ahn, C.-W.: Using policies to drive autonomic management. World of Wireless, Mobile and Multimedia Networks (2006)
6. Tibco: Goal-driven business process management: Creating agile business processes for an unpredictable environment. Tibco Whitepaper (2006)
7. Rimassa, G., Greenwood, D., Kernland, M.: The Living Systems Technology Suite: An Autonomous Middleware for Autonomic Computing. In: International Conference on Autonomic and Autonomous Systems, ICAS, Silicon Valley, USA (2006)
8. OMG, Business Process Modeling Notation, http://www.bpmn.org
9. Information Technology Infrastructure Library v3 (ITIL), http://www.itil-officialsite.com

Automated Generation of Knowledge Plane Components for Multimedia Access Networks

Steven Latré[1], Pieter Simoens[1], Wim Van de Meerssche[1],
Bart De Vleeschauwer[1], Filip De Turck[1], Bart Dhoedt[1], Piet Demeester[1],
Steven Van den Berghe[2], and Edith Gilon-de Lumley[2]

[1] IBBT - IBCN, Department of Information Technology, Ghent University, Belgium
Gaston Crommenlaan 8/201, 9050 Gent, Belgium
Tel.: +32 9 33 14 981; Fax: +32 9 33 14 899
Steven.Latre@intec.ugent.be
[2] Alcatel-Lucent Bell Labs, Copernicuslaan 50, B-2018 Antwerpen, Belgium

Abstract. The management of Quality of Experience (QoE) in the access network is largely complicated by the wide range of offered services, the myriad of possible QoE restoring actions and the increasing heterogeneity of home network configurations. The Knowledge Plane is an autonomic framework for QoE management in the access network, aiming to provide QoE management on a per user and per service basis. The Knowledge Plane contains multiple problem solving components that determine the appropriate restoring actions. Due to the wide range of possible problems and the requirement of being adaptive to new services or restoring actions, it must be possible to easily add or adapt problem solving components. Currently, generating such a problem solving component takes a lot of time and needs manual tweaking. To enable an automated generation, we present the Knowledge Plane Compiler which takes a service management objective as input, stating available monitor inputs and relevant output actions and determines a suitable neural network based Knowledge Plane incorporating this objective. The architecture of the compiler is detailed and performance results are presented.

1 Introduction

In today's broadband access networks, new added value services such as Broadcast TV, Video on Demand (VoD) and mobile thin clients are introduced. Each of these services has large service demands: they often require a considerable amount of bandwidth and only tolerate a minimum amount of packet loss, delay and jitter. In order to meet these demands, current access networks are advancing from a best-effort packet delivery to a triple-play service delivery, where the Quality of Experience (QoE: the quality as perceived by the end user) is of prime importance. Several factors are complicating the QoE management. First, the type of degradation due to network anomalies is highly dependent on the service type and the current network status. Furthermore, a myriad of techniques has been deployed in the access network, such as VLANs with bandwidth

S. van der Meer, M. Burgess, and S. Denazis (Eds.): MACE 2008, LNCS 5276, pp. 50–61, 2008.

reservation, retransmissions, erasure coding and VoD proxies. However, these techniques can only guarantee the QoE between the service originator (e.g. a video streaming server) and the access node. Most households are nowadays equipped with a comprehensive home network including wireless links, home media servers and users concurrently accessing bandwidth-intensive services.

As a result, the appropriate QoE restoring action is highly dependent on the individual situation of home network configuration, service type and network status. An autonomic framework can contribute to tackle the complexity of this individual QoE management. Our research is targeting the development of the Knowledge Plane (KPlane), an autonomic layer spanning the whole access network from service edge router up to and including the end device. It reasons on an extensive knowledge base with monitor data on the network status and the QoE of the running services. The KPlane detects decreases in QoE, e.g. due to packet loss, and determines autonomously the appropriate actions to restore the QoE, e.g. by adding redundant packets for Forward Error Correction (FEC).

Due to the wide range of problems to be solved by the KPlane, there is a need for a flexible and generic framework that adds new problem solving components or adapts existing ones when changes occur in the network or new services are offered. Manually designing these components is often not feasible. In this article, a flexible KPlane Compiler is presented, able to generate a neural network based KPlane. The operator only needs to specify the available monitor inputs, a service management objective and possible QoE restoring actions. The KPlane Compiler generates a neural network according to the specified objective.

The remainder of this architecture is structured as follows: section 2 gives an overview of the Knowledge Plane architecture. Section 3 explores related work in the field of autonomous QoE management. Section 4 presents the Knowledge Plane Compiler where problem solving components can be constructed in a flexible way. Section 5 describes the implementation details of the Knowledge Plane Compiler, while section 6 illustrates how the Knowledge Plane Compiler can aid in the QoE optimization of different use cases. Section 7 evaluates the performance of the KPlane Compiler both in construction time and correctness. Finally, section 8 concludes this paper and presents some future work.

2 KPlane Architecture

An overview of the architecture of the KPlane framework is presented in Figure 1. The Knowledge Plane is accompanied by a Monitor Plane (MPlane), comprising monitoring probes in all access network elements, an Action Plane (APlane), presenting an interface to the KPlane for the execution of the QoE restoring actions and a Knowledge Base (KBase) as an intelligent infrastructure for storing all information. More details on the functioning of the MPlane, APlane and KBase can be found in [1].

The core functionality of this architecture resides in the Knowledge Plane. Its problem solving functionality is decomposed into a three-step process, where each step analyzes the knowledge currently available and forwards its decision to

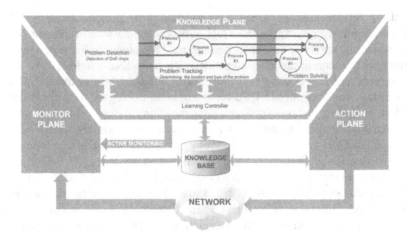

Fig. 1. Autonomous framework for the access network. This paper targets the automated generation of a specific problem solving process. For each service type, a new problem solving component can be generated.

the next component in the chain. The first step is the problem detection step: it detects suboptimal situations in the controlled network that lead to QoE drops. Detected problems are forwarded to the problem tracking step, where the problem is analyzed in more detail and the location and the cause are pinpointed. The problem tracking step then activates the appropriate problem solving components. Each problem solving component determines the best actions for a specific anomaly. Since learning capabilities are a vital part of the KPlane functionalities, the problem component should always be able to change the details of its behavior.

This paper focuses on the problem solving processes. Possible problems are specified by the operator and can be very complex and generic but can also be very specific. First, as the KPlane needs to select the best action based on the information present in the Knowledge Base, its decision making process can be very problem specific. For example, optimizing a BroadcastTV service is completely different than optimizing a mobile thin client service, where mobile thin clients execute their applications remotely and their graphics are forwarded from the server to the mobile thin client. In the first case, the KPlane needs to optimize the video quality of a multicast stream by minimizing the packet loss ratio, while in the second case the latency of a unicast stream should be optimized. Second, as the behaviour of the KPlane needs to adapt to dynamically changing environments and individual users, the KPlane needs to alter its decision making process on-line. These aspects make it difficult to construct a generic problem solving component that incorporates all the intelligence needed to tackle all services and problems that can occur in multimedia access networks. While the functionality of the MPlane, APlane and other KPlane components can be modeled in a generic way, the functionality of the problem solving component is problem specific.

The lack of a generic KPlane architecture can pose a serious challenge to constructing an autonomic architecture for QoE optimization. As no general, multi-purpose KPlane suited for all scenarios can be constructed, a new KPlane needs to be built when changes occur in the access network model (e.g. when a new service is offered to the users). The described architecture loses its autonomic behaviour if constructing such a KPlane takes a large effort to complete. Therefore, we propose, the KPlane Compiler, a novel way of constructing this KPlane based upon reinforcement learning paradigms. In this KPlane Compiler, a service provider defines an objective to optimize the network and the KPlane Compiler automatically constructs an appropriate problem solving component.

3   Related Work

The concept of a Knowledge Plane was originally presented in [2] as a layer that enables the autonomic detection and recovery of network anomalies. The Knowledge Plane concept has been applied to many different problem domains including WDM networks [3] and detecting routing changes [4]. In our work, we applied this concept to QoE optimization in an access network [5]. Furthermore, we introduced the concept of applying neural networks to implement the Knowledge Plane to enhance the QoE, together with some first results and design guidelines [6].

Reinforcement learning [7] has been successfully applied to network management problems such as QoS scheduling in wireless sensor networks [8], radio management in mesh networks [9] and resource allocation [10], [11]. In [12], reinforcement has been applied in a QoS middleware framework. However, applications must be modeled as a series of activities, which makes this framework infeasible to deploy on a network with existing services.

Adapting to changing network management objectives is also addressed in [13]. They address the key question whether a model learned from the use of one set of policies could be applied to another set of similar policies, or whether a new model must be learned from scratch as a result of run-time changes to the policies driving autonomic management. Our KPlane Compiler is complementary to this work, as it rather addresses adapting to completely new policies resulting from the availability of e.g. new QoE restoring actions.

4   KPlane Compiler

In this section, we detail our KPlane Compiler, which constructs a novel neural network based problem solving component based upon an objective defined by the service provider. While the earlier proposed KPlane performs well, it has three major limitations in its construction. First, the neural network uses a supervised learning technique to memorize its behaviour. Constructing a training set needed for supervised learning involves exhaustively trying all possible actions on all possible scenarios and selecting the action that maximized the QoE of the service as an input-output pair for the supervised learning algorithm. As will be discussed in section 7, such a brute force algorithm takes a huge amount of time to complete. A second limitation of the supervised learning approach is its inability to evaluate its decision making process. As the KPlane needs to incorporate an on-line learning mechanism to cope with changing environments, evaluating its decision making process is of key importance. When a change in environments causes errors in the decision making process, the current neural network based KPlane never detects this evolution. A third and last limitation of the current neural network based KPlane is the construction of the neural network itself, and moreover choosing the right amount of neurons in the hidden layer. Although several rules of thumb exist to choose the appropriate number of hidden neurons, this still involves manually tweaking the neural network.

These three limitations make constructing the current neural network based KPlane a time consuming task. The KPlane Compiler solves these limitations by introducing three new functions to the constructed KPlane:

- The KPlane Compiler uses a cost function instead of supervised learning to train the neural network to minimize the construction time. As will be discussed in the next section, cost function based learning algorithms still need to investigate different actions under different scenarios but the use of a brute force algorithm is avoided.
- The constructed KPlane continuously evaluates its decision making process and can trigger an on-line learning process if needed.
- Manually tuning the amount of neurons in the hidden layer of the neural network is avoided by using a specific algorithm that detects the optimal amount of hidden neurons.

The KPlane Compiler takes a network management objective and the configuration of the MPlane and APlane as input and generates a neural network based problem solving component capable of selecting the best QoE optimizing action to take given a specific configuration of the network. The KPlane Compiler can generate different KPlanes for different problem domains as long as it has the right MPlane and APlane configuration and goal to achieve. The KPlane compiler uses the information stated in the Knowledge Base as input to generate the appropriate KPlane. This information stated in the Knowledge Base is formalized through an OWL ontology; we refer to [1] for more information about the Knowledge Base.

4.1   KPlane Construction

The construction of the KPlane Compiler is detailed in Figure 2. It is initiated by the service operator by specifying three aspects of the problem as input to the KPlane Compiler. First, the service operator needs to define which *monitor values* are relevant for the problem. While the KPlane Compiler extracts all possible monitor information from the Knowledge Base, the service operator needs to select the relevant monitor parameters that can aid in detecting the cause of a QoE drop. The second piece of information the service operator needs to

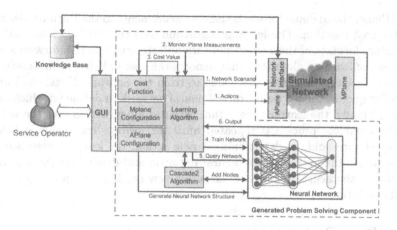

Fig. 2. Operation of the KPlane Compiler and message flow in an off-line learning process. During training of the neural network, the KPlane Compiler interacts with a NS-2 simulator to learn the optimal behaviour. During execution, the simulated network is replaced with an actual network and the network interface to the simulator is deactivated.

provide is information about which *actions to take*. Again, the KPlane Compiler uses the Knowledge Base to present all possible actions but the service operator needs to select the appropriate actions. In general, such a selection should be straightforward.

The third and most important piece of information to be presented to the KPlane Compiler is the *cost function*. This cost function defines how the service operator wants to achieve the goal of optimizing a given problem domain using the selected monitor and action information. For example, when a service operator wants to minimize the packet loss of a service, the cost function can simply be the packet loss. More complex cost functions are discussed in section 6. As this approach frees the service operator from the time consuming task of finding a suitable KPlane, the cost function enables the KPlane Compiler to achieve autonomic behaviour. Instead, the service operator defines the goal of the KPlane through the cost function and the KPlane Compiler autonomously detects which actions result in low values of the cost function and train a network that solves the problem.

Based on this information, the KPlane Compiler trains a neural network using a learning algorithm that steers the neural network based on observations made by executing actions into a real or simulated network. Conceptually, the off-line learning process works as follows. The KPlane Compiler is coupled with the simulation environment that simulates the network in which the KPlane is deployed. Both the neural and underlying network are configured based on the MPlane and APlane configuration presented by the service operator. The size of the neural network depends on the exact configuration of MPlane and APlane parameters. Next, the learning algorithm randomly generates a certain network scenario to investigate and triggers the underlying - simulated - network by executing a random action. The executed action results in new measurements performed by the MPlane, the MPlane forwards these measurements to the learning algorithm and the cost function. The learning algorithm uses this MPlane information to determine the state of the current network and the cost function forwards a cost value to the learning algorithm that denotes the cost of being in this state. The learning algorithm uses this cost value to train the network. Next, the learning controller queries the partially trained neural network to decide on which action to take. Finally, the learning algorithm executes a new action into the network and the complete process is repeated until the average cost value is below a predefined threshold. In determining a new action, the learning algorithm can choose to use the output of the neural network, and depend on the knowledge available in the neural network or execute a new random action to try and find a better solution.

4.2   KPlane Deployment

Once the performance of the neural network is satisfactory, the KPlane is coupled with an actual network as illustrated in Figure 3. In this case, construction specific components are removed and the generic components of the KPlane (i.e. the problem detection and problem tracking components) are added. During deployment, the neural network is making its decision based upon the real-life scenario occurring in the actual network. The training process, denoted in Figure 3 by (4), is temporarily halted. However, the KPlane continues to evaluate its decision making process through the cost function to enable on-line learning. If this cost function exceeds a predefined threshold, the service operator can choose to retrain the network by reactivating the training process and exploring new actions.

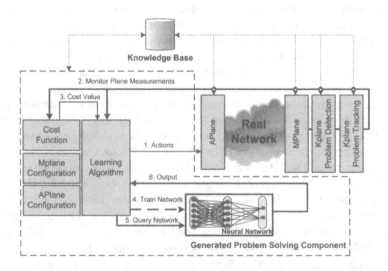

Fig. 3. Operation of the generated KPlane problem solving component and message flow during deployment. The simulated network is replaced with an actual network and the other - generic - KPlane components are added.

5   Implementation Details

In our implementation, we use a feed-forward layered neural network with as input monitor and action parameters (denoting the state of the network) and a possible action to execute. As output, the network returns the reward of executing this action into the current state. The KPlane queries the neural network by combining the current state of the network with all possible actions to execute. The action that yields the highest reward will be executed.

The neural network is modeled using the FANN [14] library improved with a reinforcement learning algorithm [15]. To construct the neural network we use the Cascade 2 [16] algorithm. In this algorithm, the neural network starts with no neurons in the hidden layer. Next, hidden neurons are trained and added to the network until the optimal amount of hidden neurons is found. This avoids manually searching for a suitable network configuration.

The implemented learning algorithm uses a reinforcement learning method, where, instead of using a training set, the neural network learns by trial-and-error. The reinforcement learning paradigm consists of an agent and an environment. At any given time t, the environment is in a state s_t. By executing an action a on the environment, the environment returns a new state s_{t+1} and a new reward r_{t+1}, defining the reward of executing a on the state s_t. The overall goal is to maximize the long-term reward by choosing the right actions. In our implementation, we used the Q-SARSA learning algorithm combined with an ϵ-greedy selection strategy where $\epsilon = 0.001$.

6   Description of Use Cases

In this section, we describe two use cases where QoE optimization can be of importance and illustrate how a suitable problem solving component can be generated by defining a cost function.

6.1   BroadcastTV Use Case

In a BroadcastTV scenario, a video is multicasted to multiple video subscribers, who watch the video in real-time. The QoE of such a scenario can be defined as the visual quality of the transmitted video. The QoE can be degraded due to packet loss caused by errors on a link or congestion. A service operator can choose to try and optimize the QoE by transmitting redundant information. A possible access network model is illustrated in Figure 4.

In this model, the KPlane resides on the access node where the QoE can be optimized on a per subscriber basis. The video server sends out different video bitrates of the same channel to cope with congestion related problems. To tackle link related losses, the video server also sends out a stream of Forward Error Correction (FEC) packets that add redundancy to the original video stream. Based on MPlane information regarding packet loss and bandwidth, the KPlane in the access node needs to determine which video bit rate to transmit and how many redundant packets to accompany with the stream.

Fig. 4. A possible access network model for a BroadcastTV scenario. The KPlane in the access node needs to the determine the optimal video bit rate and redundancy level to transmit to each subscriber.

In deciding which action to take, there is a trade-off between optimizing the packet loss and the video bitrate. The lower the video bitrate, the more redundant packets can be transmitted and the lower the chances on a congested network. However, a low video bitrate also results in a lower video quality. Therefore, a service operator needs to define a cost function where both the video bit rate is maximized and the packet loss is minimized. A possible cost function can be: $\alpha \overline{PL} - \beta \overline{BR} - \gamma \overline{FP}$ where PL is the measured packet loss after filtering the redundant FEC packets, BR is the video bitrate and FP is the amount of FEC packets. We assume that all variables are normalized between 0 and 1. This cost function favors solutions that use high video bitrates but ignores solutions that generate large levels of packet loss. Furthermore, if two solutions result in the same video bitrate and packet loss ratio the solution with the lowest levels of redundant traffic is chosen due to the last term in the equation. The values of α, β and γ illustrate the importance between the three variables and depend on the policy of the service operator. In our implementation, the values were 0.7, 0.2 and 0.1 for α, β and γ, respectively.

6.2   Mobile Thin Clients Use Case

Thin client computing is a paradigm in which the computing power is shifted from the device to a thin client server in the network. Applications are executed remotely and their graphics are relayed to the thin client over a thin client protocol. Limiting the latency is of the utmost importance, since every user event has to be transported to the thin client server before it can be processed and the resulting graphic update can be sent back to the device. The inherently time-varying nature of the wireless link and the decreasing energy level of the device battery lead to varying resource availability. The KPlane can contribute to guarantee the highest possible level of QoS in this dynamic environment.

The KPlane resides on the thin client servers, where the application graphics are encoded and sent to the client. It receives monitor information from the application, the network and the client device. Due to wireless link errors, retransmissions will occur, resulting in increased latency. This limits the user interactivity. Prioritizing the thin client traffic on the wireless link can increase the achieved throughput, but this comes at the cost of increased energy consumption. Typically, mobile thin client devices only have a limited battery autonomy. Another action can be to switch to another image transmission technology. In [17], an approach was presented to dynamically switch between a classic thin client protocol (e.g. VNC) and video streaming.

These considerations lead to the definition of the cost function: $\alpha \overline{L} + \beta \overline{T} + \gamma \overline{ECR}$. Here, L is the average latency measured between thin client server and device, T is the throughput achieved over the error-prone wireless link and ECR is a measure for the rate at which the energy level of the client device battery is decreasing. Again, the values of α, β and γ illustrate the importance between the three variables and depend on the policy of the service operator.

7 Performance Evaluation

To evaluate the performance of the KPlane Compiler we implemented the Broad-castTV use case and compared it with previous results obtained through the earlier designed neural network based reasoner using a supervised learning method' [6]. In this use case, two variables are controlled. The first one is the video bitrate which can be altered to avoid congestion or increase the visual quality. The second variable is the amount of FEC packets to cope with packet loss. Since the novel KPlane Compiler automates the generation of a KPlane, we investigated the time necessary to construct a KPlane together with the correctness of the decision making process.

7.1 Construction Time

We compared the time needed to construct both the earlier proposed, supervised learning based, KPlane and the novel, reinforcement learning based, KPlane. Tests were carried out on an AMD Athlon 2200+ 1.8Ghz machine with 512MB RAM. For the supervised learning KPlane a training set of 1200 input-output pairs was constructed. To construct this set, 40,800 different scenarios needed to be simulated and investigated. After construction of the training set, the network was trained by presenting the training set to the neural network. Details of this approach are described in [6]. This resulted in a neural network with 6 inputs, 2 outputs and 5 hidden neurons. The construction of the training set resulted in a total construction time of more than 20 days. This is considerably more than the construction time of the reinforcement learning based KPlane, where constructing the KPlane took approximately 27 hours and 34 minutes for the same problem domain. During construction, the network was trained for 30,000 episodes. In the reinforcement learning approach we obtained a network with 6 inputs, 2 outputs and 4 hidden neurons, which corresponds to the results obtained in [6].

7.2 Decision Making Process

The performance of the two KPlanes was investigated by using a NS-2 [18] based simulation topology as illustrated in figure 5. This topology resembles the use case described in section 6.1 where a video server transmits both a high quality (with an average bit rate of 2Mbps) and a low quality (with an average bit rate of 500kbps)

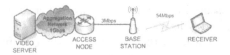

Fig. 5. Topology used to test the performance of both KPlanes. By altering the packet loss ratio, different scenarios were introduced.

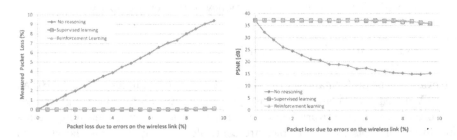

Fig. 6. Measurements of packet loss and PSNR experienced by the user for different levels of random packet loss on the wireless link. All standard deviation values are lower than 5% of the average value.

to the clients. In the investigated scenario, we varied the amount of random packet loss on the wireless link from 0% to 10%. We measured both the packet loss ratio and the PSNR, an objective video quality metric. Each test was repeated 20 times. We present average values together with the standard deviation.

The results are illustrated in Figure 6. It is clear that the performance of the decision making process of both KPlanes are almost identical. Both KPlanes succeed in minimizing the packet loss ratio by adding redundant packets to the flow when the amount of packet loss ratio increases. Also the PSNR results in almost identical values for both approaches. As the amount of packet loss on the wireless link increases, the PSNR quickly degrades when no reasoning occurs. However, when one of the two KPlanes is applied the PSNR values can be stabilized and only decreases with approximately 1dB around 10% of packet loss.

8   Conclusion and Future Work

The KPlane Compiler allows for the automatic generation of a specific problem solving component in the autonomic Knowledge Plane framework. The KPlane Compiler takes an operator objective as input to construct a neural network based KPlane using reinforcement learning. We detailed the architecture of the generated KPlane during construction and deployment and discussed how the KPlane Compiler can be effective in optimizing the QoE of two different use cases. Performance results show that the KPlane Compiler succeeds in reducing the construction time of a KPlane significantly while still maintaining the same performance in its decision making process. In future work we are targeting to extend the KPlane Compilers architecture to enable cross-service interaction and distributed behaviour between different KPlanes on different nodes. Furthermore, we will investigate how splitting the service management objective of an advanced problem into different subgoals can aid in boosting the performance of the decision making process.

References

1. Latré, S., et al.: Design of a generic knowledge base for autonomic QoE optimization in multimedia access networks. In: ACNM 2008: 2nd IEEE Workshop on Autonomic Communications for Network Management,
2. Clark, D.D., et al.: A knowledge plane for the internet. In: SIGCOMM 2003: Proceedings of the 2003 conference on Applications, technologies, architectures, and protocols for computer communications. ACM, New York (2003)
3. Urra, A., et al.: Adding new components to the knowledge plane GMPLS over WDM networks. In: IEEE Workshop on IP Operations and Management, 2004, October 11-13 (2004)
4. Teixeira, R., et al.: A measurement framework for pin-pointing routing changes. In: NetT 2004: Proceedings of the ACM SIGCOMM workshop on Network troubleshooting, pp. 313–318 (2004)
5. De Vleeschauwer, B., et al.: On the Enhancement of QoE for IPTV Services through Knowledge Plane Deployment. In: Broadband Europe (2006)
6. Simoens, P., et al.: Design of an autonomic QoE reasoner for improving access network performance. In: Fourth International Conference on Autonomic and Autonomous Systems, 2008. ICAS 2008 (2008)
7. Sutton, R., et al.: Reinforcement Learning: An Introduction. MIT Press, Cambridge (1998)
8. Ouferhat, N., et al.: A qos scheduler packets for wireless sensor networks. In: IEEE/ACS International Conference on Computer Systems and Applications, 2007. AICCSA 2007, May 13-16 (2007)
9. Niyato, D., et al.: Radio resource management in mimo-ofdm- mesh networks: Issues and approaches. IEEE Communications Magazine (2007)
10. Vengerov, D.: A reinforcement learning approach to dynamic resource allocation. Engineering Applications of Artificial Intelligence 20(3), 383–390 (2007)
11. Tesauro, G., et al.: On the use of hybrid reinforcement learning for autonomic resource allocation. Cluster Computing 10(3), 287–299 (2007)
12. Vienne, P., et al.: A middleware for autonomic QoS management based on learning. In: SEM 2005: Proceedings of the 5th international workshop on Software engineering and middleware, pp. 1–8. ACM, New York (2005)
13. Bahati, R.M., et al.: Adapting to run-time changes in policies driving autonomic management. In: Fourth International Conference on Autonomic and Autonomous Systems, 2008. ICAS 2008, March 16-21, pp. 88–93 (2008)
14. Fast artificial neural network library (fann), http://leenissen.dk/fann/
15. Nissen, S.: Large scale reinforcement learning using q-sarsa and cascading neural networks. M.Sc. Thesis (October 2007)
16. Fahlman, S.E. et al.: The cascade 2 learning architecture. technical report cmu-cs-tr-96-184, carnegie mellon university
17. De Winter, D., et al.: A hybrid thin-client protocol for multimedia streaming and interactive gaming applications. In: Proceedings of Network and Operating Systems Support for Digital Audio and Video 2006 (NOSSDAV 2006), pp. 86–92 (2006)
18. Ns-2, The Network Simulator, http://www.isi.edu/nsnam/ns/

Model-Driven Adaptive Self-healing for Autonomic Computing

Yan Liu, Jing Zhang, and John Strassner

Motorola Labs, Schaumburg, IL 60193, USA
{yanliu,j.zhang,john.strassner}@motorola.com

Abstract. Self-healing is a vital property that an autonomic system must possess in order to provide robust performance and survivability. The promise of self-healing depends on other properties that the system should provide, which include self-monitoring and self-configuring. Autonomic systems further require self-healing behavior to adapt to changes in user needs, business goals, and environmental conditions such that self-healing decisions are made dynamically and adaptively according to the system context. In this paper, we propose a model-driven approach that leverages modeling techniques, reliability engineering methodologies, and aspect-oriented development to realize an adaptive self-healing paradigm for autonomic computing.

1 Introduction

When applied to computer-based systems and networks, self-healing is one aspect of the set of capabilities exhibited by autonomic computational systems that are often represented by the phrase self-*. These include features such as self-protecting, self-configuring, self-healing, and self-optimizing [1]. A self-healing system is one that has the ability to discover, diagnose, and repair (or at least mitigate) disruptions to the services it delivers. Autonomic systems further extend this notion of self-healing to include the capabilities to adapt to changes in the environment (for example, to maintain its performance or availability of resources).

For large scale systems, many different types of faults may exist, and their differing natures often require disparate, tailored approaches to detect, let alone fix. Hence, for those systems, self-healing behavior includes the use of multiple types of detection, diagnosis, and repair mechanisms. In autonomic computing, these self-healing activities involved in any healing operations should be optimized and adapted to changing system context. This requires an autonomic system to make self-healing decisions adaptively, which include when to invoke self-healing (prediction, detection and identification), what self-healing mechanism to be invoked (analysis and diagnosis), and how to heal the system effectively and efficiently (report or rejuvenate or recover). Such a decision making process for intelligent self-healing is characterized by not only flexibility but also adaptivity.

The concept of self-healing is built around the notion that the risk raised by a failure varies over time in a changing system context. At the component level, for the same type of failure, the location of the failure also has a direct impact on its projected risk. For

S. van der Meer, M. Burgess, and S. Denazis (Eds.): MACE 2008, LNCS 5276, pp. 62–73, 2008.

example, a timeout failure of a critical component running a computationally intensive algorithm could be catastrophic and must be dealt with immediately; whereas a timeout failure of a low priority communication could be ignored completely. The decision to be made on failure mediation strategy is inevitably affected by the system context involving time, location, and relevant events. In order for the system to obtain the best decision in a dynamic environment, an adaptive healing scheme must be adopted to detect not only the failures, but also the system context. This enables the system to react properly to different failures according to a particular context, and provide feedback to the system for improvement of its self-healing behavior.

In this paper, we propose a model-driven self-healing approach that is designed to adapt to changing user needs, business goals, and environmental conditions. We apply an adaptive control loop to collect failures and their contextual information, analyze these information, decide the best mediation strategy, and invoke the corresponding failure mitigator to complete the self-healing process. We employ a combination of object-oriented adaptation and process-oriented adaptation, and leverage the advantages of various modeling techniques to realize the control loop. The failures and self-healing mechanisms can be modeled and specified using UML. The detector and analyzer can be specified and modeled as aspects to be separated from the main functions of the monitored system. The online decision making can be supported by reliability modeling using methods and tools that have a record of successful applications in the literature of reliability engineering. According to the decisions, the healing actions are then invoked by instantiating the aspects for failure mitigation and executed by dynamic aspect weaving. Thus, we define an adaptable self-healing approach for autonomic systems, where the failure mediation strategy for self-healing can be adaptively selected according to system context and dynamically invoked during run-time execution.

The rest of the paper is structured as follows. Section 2 describes the need for adaptation in self-healing behavior for autonomic systems and introduces an adaptive control scheme to realize the proposed adaptive paradigm. Section 3 describes the models for failure specification to support adaptive failure mediation. Section 4 discusses the candidate techniques and methods that can be leveraged to facilitate the adaptive healing approach. Section 5 concludes the paper.

2   An Adaptive Approach

Self-awareness is fundamentally necessary for supporting the adaptive behavior of complex systems, since the knowledge of both expected and unexpected behavior are used to help define the adaptive actions for the correct and safe behavior as well as deviations from such behavior. Environmental awareness is manifested as two additional capabilities: self-monitoring and self-configuring. These processes - self-awareness, self-monitoring, and self-configuring - are required to enable self-healing capabilities provide rapid recovery and recuperation against system failures to support survivability and reliability enhancements in system operation. The self-monitoring aspect of self-healing is manifested by the ability to detect failures and their contextual information while self-configuring is characterized by the invocation or generation of the proper healing actions.

2.1 Software Failures and Healing Mechanisms

It is a common finding in reliability engineering that a failure that occurs at different times during the lifespan of a software can have different meanings and thus requires different remedies. A failure occurring at an early stage in its lifecycle, as illustrated in Figure 1, is likely to be detected by testing and fixed or removed by debugging. At this stage, preventive self-healing mechanisms can be employed for critical components in order to protect against one or more failure conditions that have been identified as failure triggers. This usually involves methods such as wrappers and proxies for mostly generic failures, such as core dump failures caused by buffer overflows, timeout failures for communication, and so forth. After the system is deployed, the maintenance of a system would rely heavily on feedback from its users which would be used by the developers to upgrade the software to eliminate the faults that have caused the failures. At this stage, statically specified self-healing actions behave as intended and continue repairing the system from failures that were already known. Previously defined healing actions can be updated and new healing actions could be added when a new failure is reported and its mediation strategy is modified or defined. Depending on how the system reacts to a failure or a set of failures, the healing actions will be adjusted accordingly. The adjustment of self-healing behavior becomes particularly important when the software ages over time. Generic software failures as well as domain-specific failures that might have escaped from testing will have an accumulative effect on system operation. A self-healing action that initially only requires reporting and logging might be interpreted as an integral part of a severe failure. Rejuvenation could be taken at this point to restart the service before the situation worsens. Nevertheless, there will be times where certain failures are beyond rejuvenation and their consequences can only be mitigated by failure quarantine/removal as part of the system recovery.

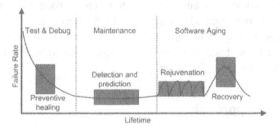

Fig. 1. Software Failure Rate Over Time

The system context also has a major impact on how the system should heal. Figure 2 illustrates the operational domains for such an adaptivity need. The operational domain of a system can be viewed as a space divided into different regions reflecting the possible states of a system in terms of reliability, which include reliable behavior, failure-prone behavior, and failure. For most well designed systems, there are a set of high-level goals that the system must maintain regardless of the environmental conditions. The realization of these goals ensures that the system will remain in a "safe region". Rigorous testing is usually conducted on critical components for system verification and validation before the system is deployed. While non-critical goals might be

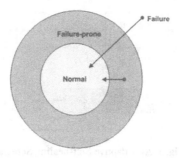

Fig. 2. Operational Domains for Self-healing

relaxed or overlooked, failures caused by such relaxation still have a negative impact on system operation that might possibly lead to system failure. Some of these failures might even become fatal given an extreme system context. Presumably, there are clearly defined failures that are known to be hazardous to system functions and put the system operation into an abnormal region. Operating in an abnormal region would certainly result in a system failure. In between, the system functions that are affected by the accumulative impact of failure(s) over time in a changing system context are subjected to potential system failure. This is when we consider the system is operating in a region where the operations are considered failure-prone. In such a state, it is predicted that a failure could be imminent or "likely". The determination of system state and prediction of its transition probability can be modeled and calculated with the aide of reliability models [2].

2.2 An Adaptive Self-healing Scheme

There exist a number of approaches that employ on-line monitoring techniques for failure detection and identification, followed by failure resolution external to the monitored system. Projects in the DARPA DASADA program [3] describe an architecture that uses probes and gauges to monitor the execution of programs, generate events containing measurements, and take actions based on the interpretation of events. Effectors interact with the system to ensure that system's run-time behavior fits within the envelope of acceptable behavior. Authors in [4] propose the generation of proxies and wrappers to add autonomic functionalities to object-oriented applications to cope with failures without source code adaptation. The IEEE Standard Classification for Software Anomalies [5] provides a comprehensive list of software anomaly classification and related data items that are helpful to identify and track anomalies. The methodology of this standard is based on a process (sequence of steps) that pursues a logical progression from the initial recognition of an anomaly to its final disposition. Although some of the issues with software failures can be tackled using service replication as proposed by the authors in [6], adaptable on-line monitoring and self-healing approaches are yet rarely defined for software failures simply because the risks of many software failures can only be projected and their mitigation strategy be dynamically invoked during run-time execution.

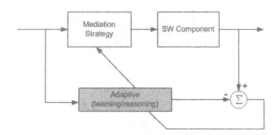

Fig. 3. An Adaptive Self-healing Scheme

We propose an adaptive feedback control loop to realize adaptive self-healing behavior as depicted by Figure 3. The key activities that are performed in the control loop are collect, analyze, decide, and act. Learning and reasoning functions act as the intelligent component of the loop that carries out the main functionality of "analyzing" to support dynamic decision making. Analytical models, such as those for reliability modeling [2], as well as empirical knowledge can be applied to analyze the current system context. By calculating the risks to reliable operation for a specific context, the system can suggest a particular mediation strategy to use to fix the erroneous software component. The feedback of these actions provide useful information for the system to adjust its mediation strategy and tune the performance of the control loop. By applying the adaptive control loop, adaptive self-healing behavior is then characterized by reliable context-ware failure detection and its ability to invoke the best healing strategy as a response to the failure and its context.

Techniques for adaptability can be divided into different categories based on how adaptation is realized [7]. There are three main approaches to consider. Model-driven architectural adaptation models the environment and the adaptation, and modifies the model to represent any changes in how the system adapts. This approach uses modeling to analyze, design, and implement the system. Object-oriented adaptation uses the model to analyze and design actions to be taken, but only modifies the objects that perform the actions at runtime. Process-oriented adaptation accomplishes adaptation by defining processes that generate the objects and methods that are needed for adaptation. In our approach, we take advantage of the second and third methods to offer a combined solution; we use object-oriented adaptation for failure specification and process-oriented adaptation for adaptive failure mediation. We first specify the targeted objects (failures in this case) through the help of modeling techniques. Then, for adaptation of the actions to be taken on these objects, we follow the process-oriented approach to enable dynamic generation of mediation strategies using an aspect-oriented mechanism, which enables mediation strategies to be modeled as aspects and dynamically generated and executed through dynamic aspect weaving. Above all, techniques that can be used to achieve prompt and accurate detection and analysis of the system context are essential to support any adaptable healing strategy. Fortunately, a rich literature in reliability modeling provides effective means in interpreting and predicting the system context, thereby allowing the model-based dynamic aspects to be applied to enable adaptive self-healing.

3 Model-Based Failure Specification and Healing Mechanisms

One of the ultimate goals of software engineering is to construct software that is easily modified and extended. A desired result is to achieve modularization such that a change in a design decision is centralized to one location [8]. Our experience has led us to believe that model driven software development and maintenance is a promising approach to support modularization and enable more efficient self-healing [9]. Model-based designs can support well-defined self-healing behavior specification, while adaptive software development methods provide feasible and flexible solutions to implement self-healing functionality. Furthermore, techniques such as aspect-oriented development and dynamic aspect development can be exploited to separate self-healing concerns from the main functions and enable real-time instantiation of adaptive operations.

Figure 4 shows a general model representation for software failures and self-healing mechanisms. Different types of failures may be present for software, which is modeled as either an atomic software component or a composite of software component(s) [10]. A software failure can be detected by one or more different types of detectors; failures are then analyzed by one or more failure analyzers. More than one failure might be analyzed by an analyzer to discover the relationships among these failures and help better characterize these failures and their underlying root causes. A failure analyzer also predicts and/or determines the risk raised by the failure(s). In accordance with the different extents of damage that a failure might bring to the system, the mitigator invokes different failure mediation strategies and takes different sets of actions that transform the software from its failure state to a specified operational state [11].

A number of software failure classifications are defined in the reliability engineering literature. Some of them simply classify failures into different types based on their risk levels, while others focus on the causes of the failures. In our proposed self-healing framework for failure detection and mitigation, we need a classification that can be used to effectively categorize the failures while stressing the domain specific constraints and operation critical requirements that a failure impacts. This is consistent with Pumfrey's

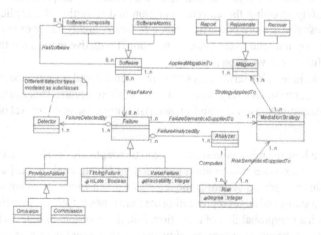

Fig. 4. The Model of Failure, Risk, and Mitigation

classification of failures [12], which considers the component or system as the provider of a service or a set of services, each consisting of a particular type of value delivered within a defined interval. The model shown in Figure 4 specifies Pumfrey's categories of software failures that may occur: provision failures, timing failures, and value failures.

- Provision Failure. Both omission failures and commission failures are considered provision failures, as the former indicates no service is delivered while the latter delivers services that are not required.
- Timing Failure. This includes late or early delivery of service. The timing failure is usually associated with certain time constraints, which can be a real time constraint or a relative deadline with respect to certain events. For example, a time limit can be imposed on the alarm correlation process in a fault management system, as opposed to the relative deadline which states that "the alarm correlation must be completed before the next batch of alarms is received".
- Value Failure. This type of failure is defined by the incorrect value provided by the service.

Each type of failure requires its specific failure detectors. The effects of such failures can be divided into three categories based on their risk index assigned by the analyzer: insignificant, moderate, and significant. Although most methods proposed and used for failure risk analyses are mainly analytical, thresholds and criteria for such divisions are very domain specific and usually obtained empirically.This implies that certain adaptive behavior, such as learning and reasoning, is needed to support the decision making process. Similarly, the invocation of failure mediation strategies also requires adaptivity. In our proposed model, based on the notion of self-healing, we divide the existing mediation strategies into three categories: report, rejuvenate, and recover.

- Report. When the risk of a failure is considered insignificant (i.e., it will not affect the normal operations of the system), it is only required that such a failure be reported and recorded. No immediate action is necessary in this case.
- Rejuvenate. Software rejuvenation, defined by Huang et. al. [13], resolves the failure by safely stopping the current operation and restarting the application. This strategy usually is more powerful when a failure is highly likely or present that is hazardous yet not fatal to the system operation. Predictive models are thus particularly useful for rejuvenation actions.
- Recover. Rejuvenation terminates software execution and restarts it before a failure occurs. In contrast, recovery is needed after a failure occurs. This usually includes failure quarantine/masking, consequence/risk mitigation, and removal of the causal faults.

To illustrate how the mitigation strategies can be adaptively decided, we use the transition model for software rejuvenation proposed by Huang et.al. in [13] as shown in Figure 5. In this research, a system is modeled as a graph where states are used to capture the system status and edges representing the transitions between states. Every edge is associated with a rate/probability of transition. Initially, a system in state S_0 is functioning as required. If the system supports rejuvenation, then over time a system transitions from S_0 to S_p with rate R_0. In state S_p, the system is considered to be in an unstable

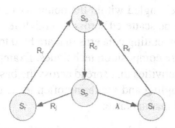

Fig. 5. Transition Model for Software with Rejuvenation

state; note that it has not reached the failed state, S_f. While in state S_p, the system has two possible actions given the nature of the failures and the system context. It can either take a rejuvenation action to go through S_r in an attempt to return to S_0 or, if the risks posed by the failures possible in this particular system context are considered too high, then the only path the system can take to return to S_0 is through failure recovery (S_f). Since a number of methods exist that provide reasonably reliable solutions to estimate model parameters, the transition model can be used as an effective means to support the adaptive selection of a mediation strategy from the above listed three categories of mitigation actions. Note that Figure 4 defines a model that can be extended or used as is. However, the failure rate needs to be estimated for a model to be used for a given system. For instance, if we assume that the failure rate is an exponential distribution, then we can build a set of differential equations for these rates using that failure distribution.

4 Model-Driven Aspect-Oriented Self-healing Adaptation

The previous sections describe the model-based approaches to model, analyze, and predict failures for self-healing. However, for any type of autonomic system, of which self-healing is a must-have capability, the static adaptation strategy that is designed to handle failures upon certain statically defined events cannot suffice the needs for dynamic adaptation. As the system evolves, the same type of failure occurs in different contexts could imply different magnitude of risks and thus requires different mediation strategy. To realize adaptive self-healing, the actions to be taken on the failures and their related objects must be adapted accordingly. This motivates us to investigate the dynamic generation of mediation strategies using an aspect-oriented mechanism, which enables mediation strategies to be modeled as aspects and dynamically generated and executed through dynamic aspect weaving.

4.1 Model-Driven Aspect-Orientation

Most existing model-driven self-healing approaches rely on modeling techniques to specify the healing behavior in design time as part of the system activity models. Activity modeling, as one of the main UML techniques for specification of the behavioral aspects of a system, is often applied to document workflows in a system, e.g., the logic of a single operation, the scenario of a use case, or the flow logic of a business process. Due to the increasing complexity of software systems, activity models may involve numerous activities that are tangled within the boundary of a single module. In other cases, a single activity may be scattered across several different activity modules. Such activities are defined as crosscutting concerns that are hard to modularize into separate units using existing software composition techniques. Examples are timeout monitors, logging or error handling activities that spread across the base functionality of the system. The occurrence of tangling and scattering often leads to several impediments to system comprehension and maintenance:

– Discovering or understanding the representation of a specific crosscutting concern that is spread over the system hierarchy is difficult, because the concern is not localized in one single module. This limits the ability to reason analytically about such a concern.
– Changing concerns to reflect changing requirements is also difficult and time consuming, because the engineers must go into each relevant module and modify the specific elements one by one. The change process is error-prone and affects productivity and correctness [14].

Aspect-oriented software development (AOSD) [15] offers a powerful technology for handling such concerns, whereby the crosscutting is explicitly specified as an *aspect*. An aspect-oriented extension can be applied to activity modeling for encapsulating crosscutting concerns into the constructs of aspects, which are systematically integrated with (a.k.a., woven into) the base activities by an underlying aspect weaver. Motorola has previously developed an industry-strength weaver for enabling aspect-oriented weaving for UML statecharts as well as activity models [16]. The goal is to provide designers with more coherent and manageable activity modules through the clean separation of concerns. Such an aspect-oriented approach offers the fundamental support to self-healing adaptation by separating the dynamic and adaptive self-healing activities, expected or unexpected, which are involved in healing activity specification as dictated by the above-mentioned failure models.

4.2   Two-Step Aspect Weaving

Adaptive mediation is characterized by its ability to analyze the failures followed by dynamically determining the most appropriate remedy and applying that remedy to mitigate the risks. We propose an aspect-oriented approach as depicted in Figure 6 to realize adaptive mediation. It contains two steps of aspect weaving: the first step uses static weaving of the base system and failure detector/analyzer; and the second step uses runtime dynamic weaving of the instrumented system and failure mitigators.

As mentioned in Section 3, failure detectors and analyzers are intended to capture anomalous status of the software system and analyze the risk of the failure, so as to provide adaptive mediation strategies for self-healing. In this sense, failure detectors and analyzers can be encapsulated in static aspects and woven into the base system before runtime. Figure 7 shows an example of an aspect activity model for detecting and analyzing timeout failure. The *proceed* action refers to any activity that has sensitive timing concerns and needs to be analyzed upon the timeout failure. The aspect model intercepts and wraps the *proceed* activity and a timer with an interruptible activity region (denoted as a dashed rectangle with rounded corners), which represents that

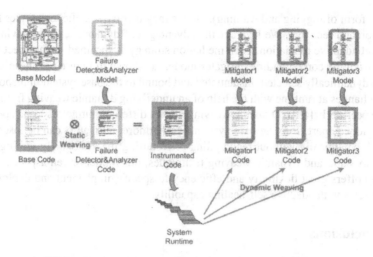

Fig. 6. Model-driven Aspect-oriented Self-healing Adaptation

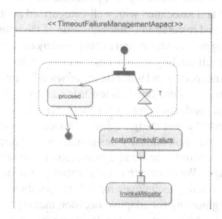

Fig. 7. Timeout Failure Detector and Analyzer Aspect Model

whenever the flow leaves the region via interrupting edges, all of the activities in the region will be terminated. Specifically, if the *proceed* activity completes execution successfully before it runs out of time, the control of the flow will return to the base process (via the bull's eye symbol) and continue with the next activity that follows the *proceed* action. Otherwise, the *proceed* process will be shut down properly and a timeout failure will be captured and passed to the failure analyzer (a detailed specification of the failure analyzer is omitted here due to the space limitation). The failure detector/analyzer model is used to derive or generate source code specified in an aspect language (e.g., AspectJ [17]), which is in turn integrated with the base code through a static weaver (e.g., AspectJ weaver). The result is an instrumented system that contains the capability of failure detection and analyzing.

Based on the different system context during runtime, different mediation strategies can be applied for the same failure. Some of these mediation activities are generic (e.g., report in form of logging and warning). Others may involve specific techniques for rejuvenation and recovery. We leverage the advantages of dynamic aspect weaving [18] to support adaptive mediation. Each mediation strategy is specified in an aspect that is derived from the corresponding mitigator model (as shown in Figure 6). These aspects are then dynamically selected, instantiated and bound to the base system in response to context changes at runtime with the help of an underlying dynamic weaving framework (e.g., AspectWerkz[19]). Dynamic weaving allows different mitigators to be specified and developed apart from the base system. Furthermore, mitigators can be inserted or removed dynamically without recompiling or restarting the system. By uniting modeling with static and dynamic weaving techniques, our model-driven aspect-oriented approach offers great flexibility and efficiency to specify, implement and deploy software systems with adaptive self-healing capability.

5   Conclusions

It has been proposed in the past that self-healing could be designed into system architecture to improve the system reliability and performance [20]. A number of generic failures are pre-defined and associated with well-categorized faults and then addressed by detection, isolation, and restoration. Although some of the issues with software failures can be tackled using service replication as proposed by the authors in [6], adaptable on-line monitoring and self-healing approaches are rarely defined for software failures simply because many unexpected and unforeseen software failures can only be detected during run-time execution. Related research towards adaptive self-healing still focuses on the architectural styles and requirements for adaptable self-healing capabilities [21], providing a solution from system design using architectural description languages or modeling techniques. Instead of statically designing and architecting for self-healing, we propose an adaptive control scheme to dynamically adapt self-healing behavior to system contextual changes. We demonstrate the feasibility of such an adaptive paradigm by using the existing modeling techniques for failure specification, leveraging the advances of reliability engineering for adaptive decision making, and accomplishing the adaptive failure mediation by aspect-oriented development.

Our future work will be focused on exploring the proposed methods to support self-healing capability for real-world systems. We will also deploy policy directed self-* capabilities in the context of model based policy based autonomic networking systems [22], for instance, specifying and modeling policies at high levels and then mapping them with various parameters and constraints for adaptive self-healing operations, all of which will be based on more general and advanced techniques for failure prediction, classification, reasoning, and intelligent strategy selection for failure mediation.

References

1. Kephart, J.O., Chess., D.M.: The vision of autonomic computing. IEEE Computer 36(1) (2003)
2. Musa, J.: Software Reliability Engineered Testing. McGraw-Hill, Inc., New York (1998)
3. Parekh, J., Kaiser, G., Gross, P., Valetto, G.: Retrofitting autonomic capabilities onto legacy systems. Cluster Computing 9(2), 141–159 (2006)

 4. Haydarlou, A.R., Overeinder, B.J., Brazier, F.M.T.: A self-healing approach for object-oriented applications. In: Proceedings of Sixteenth International Workshop on Database and Expert Systems Applications, pp. 191–195 (2005)
 5. Sterritt, R., Hinchey, M.G.: Autonomicity - an antidote for complexity?, 283–291 (2005)
 6. Guerraoui, R., Schiper, A.: Software-based replication for fault tolerance. Computer 30(4), 68–74 (1997)
 7. Simon, A.: The Science of the Artificial. MIT Press, Cambridge (1981)
 8. Parnas, D.L.: On the criteria to be used in decomposing systems into modules. Commun. ACM 15(12), 1053–1058 (1972)
 9. Liu, Y., Zhang, J., Jiang, M., Raymer, D., Strassner, J.: A model-based approach to adding autonomic capabilities to network fault management system. In: Proceedings of the IEEE/IFIP Network Operations and Management Symposium 2008, Salvardo, Brazil (2008)
10. Strassner, J.: Policy-Based Network Management: Solutions for the Next Generation. The Morgan Kaufmann Series in Networking. Morgan Kaufmann Publishers Inc., San Francisco (2003)
11. Ermagan, V., Mizutani, J.i., Oguchi, K., Weir, D.: Towards model-based failure-management for automotive software. In: SEAS 2007: Proceedings of the 4th International Workshop on Software Engineering for Automotive Systems, p. 8. IEEE Computer Society, Washington (2007)
12. Pumfrey, D.J.: The principled design of computer system safety analyses. Department of Computer Science, University of York, PhD Thesis (2000)
13. Huang, Y., Kintala, C., Kolettis, N., Fulton, N.D.: Software rejuvenation: analysis, module and applications. In: Twenty-Fifth International Symposium on Fault-Tolerant Computing, FTCS-25. Digest of Papers, vol. 30, pp. 381–390 (1995)
14. Gray, J., Lin, Y., Zhang, J.: Automating change evolution in model-driven engineering. IEEE Computer 39(2), 51–58 (2006)
15. Aspect-oriented software development, http://www.aosd.net/
16. Zhang, J., Liu, Y., Jiang, M., Strassner, J.: An aspect-oriented approach to handling crosscutting concerns in activity modeling. In: IAENG International Conference on Software Engineering (ICSE 2008), pp. 885–890 (2008)
17. Kiczales, G., Hilsdale, E., Hugunin, J., Kersten, M., Palm, J., Griswold, W.: Getting started with aspect. Communications of ACM 44(10), 59–65 (2001)
18. Popovici, A., Gross, T., Alonso, G.: Dynamic weaving for aspect-oriented programming. In: AOSD 2002: Proceedings of the 1st international conference on Aspect-oriented software development, p. 141. ACM, New York (2002)
19. Aspectwerkz - dynamic aop for java, http://aspectwerkz.codehaus.org/
20. Fujisaki, T., Hamada, M., Kageyama, K.: A scalable fault-tolerant network management system built using distributed object technology. In: EDOC 1997: Proceedings of the 1st International Conference on Enterprise Distributed Object Computing, pp. 140–148. IEEE Computer Society, Washington (1997)
21. Mikic-Rakic, M., Mehta, N., Medvidovic, N.: Architectural style requirements for self-healing systems. In: WOSS 2002: Proceedings of the first workshop on Self-healing systems, pp. 49–54. ACM Press, New York (2002)
22. Raymer, D., Strassner, J., Lehtihet, E., van der Meer, S.: End-to-end model driven policy based network management. In: POLICY 2006: Proceedings of the Seventh IEEE International Workshop on Policies for Distributed Systems and Networks (POLICY 2006), pp. 67–70. IEEE Computer Society, Washington (2006)

Self-organising Management Overlays for Future Internet Services

Lawrence Cheng[1], Alex Galis[1], Bertrand Mathieu[2], Kerry Jean[1], Roel Ocampo[1,3],
Lefteris Mamatas[1], Javier Rubio-Loyola[4], Joan Serrat[4], Andreas Berl[5],
Hermann de Meer[5], Steven Davy[6], Zeinab Movahedi[7], and Laurent Lefevre[8]

[1] University College London, UK
`{a.galis,l.cheng,k.jean,r.ocampo,l.mamatas}@ee.ucl.ac.uk`
[2] France Telecom, France
`bertrand2.mathieu@orange-ftgroup.com`
[3] University of the Philippines, Philippines
`roel@eee.upd.edu.ph`
[4] Universitat Politècnica de Catalunya, Spain
`{jrloyola,serrat}@tsc.upc.edu`
[5] University of Passau, Germany
`{andreas.berl,demeer}@uni-passau.de`
[6] Waterford Institute of Technology, Ireland
`sdavy@tssg.org`
[7] Université Pierre et Marie Curie, France
`zeinab.movahedi@lip6.fr`
[8] INRIA RESO, University of Lyon, France
`laurent.lefevre@ens-lyon.fr`

Abstract. Networks are becoming service-aware implying that all relevant business goals pertaining to a service are fulfilled, and also the network resources are used optimally. Future Internet Networks (FIN) have time varying topology (e.g. such networks are envisaged in Autonomic Internet [1], FIND program [2], GENI program [3], FIRE program [4], Ambient Networks [5], Adhoc networks [6]) and service availability and service context change as nodes join and leave the networks. In this paper we propose and evaluate a new self-organising service management system that manages such changes known as the Overlay Management Backbones (OMBs). The OMB is a self-organising solution to the problem space in which each OMB node is dynamically assigned a different service context task. The selection of OMB nodes is conducted automatically, without the need of relatively heavy-weighted dynamic negotiations. Our solution relies on the scalability and dynamicity advantages of Distributed Hash Tables (DHTs). This system is needed to select continuously, automatically, and dynamically a set of network nodes, to become responsible for collecting the availability information of service context in the changing network. This solution advances the state of the art avoiding dynamic negotiations between all network nodes reducing management complexity and cost for bandwidth-limited environments.

Keywords: Self-organised management, Autonomic Internet, Distributed hash tables, Peer-to-Peer.

S. van der Meer, M. Burgess, and S. Denazis (Eds.): MACE 2008, LNCS 5276, pp. 74–89, 2008.
© Springer-Verlag Berlin Heidelberg 2008

1 Introduction

Recently, the use of structured and unstructured Peer-to-Peer (P2P) networks for supporting multimedia services in the Internet, such as P2P streaming, has attracted a great deal of attention. Unstructured P2P networks, such as Gnutella [7], BitTorrent [8], Freenet [9], and more, organise peers in a random graph in flat or hierarchical manners (e.g. SuperPeers layer) [10]. In contrast, structured P2P networks, such as Content Addressable Networks (CANs) [11], Pastry [12], Chord [13], and more, assign keys to peers, organising them and mapping data items to such keys. However, the possibility of utilising the scalable and decentralisation features of P2P techniques [14] for solving service management challenges in large-scale, heterogeneous networks with time varying topology such as Future Internet Networks (FINs) has not been fully realised.

FINs consist of nodes that are heterogeneous end user devices such as mobile phones, MP3 players, PDAs, servers, etc., that are sharing services through wired or bandwidth-limited channels. FIN nodes [1][2][3] are dynamic, that they may join in and leave a service domain (i.e. P2P services, connectivity services, etc) at any time. Services reside on nodes; thus, as nodes join and leave the network, service availability in the network changes. The major challenge in developing a common control space for service management in dynamically changing, bandwidth-limited networks is to identify the availability of different types of services that are currently available to end users. Note that an end user service may be implemented by composing several services.

In order to determine the availability of different types of services in the network, as with WebServices [15], a consistent and distributed context service directory is needed. This service directory should be distributed allowing the system to be scalable. This paper presents a novel protocol, known as the Overlay Management Backbones (OMBs), which assigns different service availability monitoring tasks to peers in a dynamically changing network in an automatic and self-organising manner [16] hence the title of this paper. This protocol involves selecting and continuously maintaining a set of nodes in the network to act as distributed service directories. These service directories keep track of the different types of services that are currently available in the network, and are able to re-direct consumers or other management entities to access the services that are needed to implement more tailor-made service(s) that consumers want. Our solution achieves these goals, by utilising structured P2P systems i.e. Distributed Hash Tables (DHTs).

The Section 2 of this paper provides background information of the concepts addressed in this paper. Section 3 describes the OMB protocol and Section 4 presents some evaluation results. Finally Section 5 concludes the paper and gives some further work.

2 Background

2.1 Views on Autonomic Internet /Future Internet Networks

Networks are becoming service-aware. Service awareness means not only that all digital items pertaining to a service are delivered but also that all business or other relations pertaining to a service offer are fulfilled and the network resources are optimally used in the service delivery. In addition, the network's design is moving towards a different level of automation and self-management. The solution envisaged in [1][17] is based upon an optimised network and service layers solution which guarantees built-in orchestrated reliability, robustness, mobility, context, access, security, service support and self-management of the communication resources and services. It suggests a transition from a service agnostic Internet to service-aware network, managing resources by applying Autonomic principles as depicted in Figure 1. In order to achieve the objective of service-aware resources and to overcome the ossification of the current Internet, [1][17] aims to develop a self-managing virtual resource overlay that can span across heterogeneous networks and that supports service mobility, security, quality of service and reliability. In this overlay network, multiple virtual networks could co-exist on top of a shared substrate with uniform control. Ambient networking [5] addresses also the needs of future mobile and wireless systems as well as providing innovative solutions for "fixed-mobile convergence". The main feature of an Ambient Network is an Ambient Control Space (ACS), which can be used to integrate and interoperate seamlessly any existing networks [18][5].

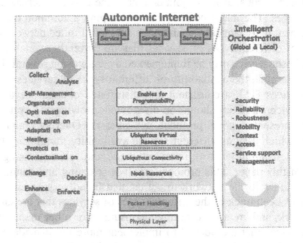

Fig. 1. Autonomic Internet

2.2 Requested Features: Self-management and Context-Awareness

Currently, network management faces many challenges: complexity, data volume, data comprehension, changing rules, reactive monitoring, resource availability, and others. Self-management research started in 1989 [16] and it aims to automatically perform these tasks. The first main aim of Self-management systems is that they manage complexity, possess self-knowledge, continuously tune themselves, adapt to unpredictable conditions, prevent and recover from failures and provide a safe environment [19][20]. The second main aim [19] of Self-management systems is that they exhibit self-awareness properties, in particular self - optimisation; - organisation; - configuration; -adaptation/contextualisation; - healing; - protection.

On the other hand, the term "context aware" was first used in [21], which referred context as locations, identities of nearby people and objects and changes to those objects. In [22], the term of context was defined as locations, identities of the people around the user, the time of day, season, temperature, etc. Other refinements of the definition consider aspects of context [23] like: where you are, who you are, and what resources are nearby. In [24], context was defined to be the subset of physical and conceptual states of interest to a particular entity. One key definition for service context was espoused in [25] and can be adapted for this paper as service or network context "*Any information, obtained implicitly or explicitly, that can be used to characterise the situation of an entity involved in an application or service, especially the information that refers to the constantly changing environment of an entity. That information must be relevant to a service or application. An entity can be a physical object such as a person, a mobile host, a physical link, or a virtual object such as an application, process or computational object that is relevant to the application or service involved*". Network context characteristics include i. Network description (e.g. network identity, location, access-types, coverage); ii. Network resources in general (e.g. bandwidth, supported services, available media ports for media conversion, available Quality of Service (QoS), security levels provisioned); iii. Flow context characteristics: flows are a possible embodiment of the interaction between the user and networks [26]. Context information that characterizes these flows may be used to optimise or enhance this interaction including: the state of the links and nodes that transport the flow, such as congestion level, latency/jitter/loss/error rate, media characteristics, reliability, security; the capabilities of the end-devices; the activities, intentions, preferences or identities of the users; or the nature and state of the end-applications that produce or consume the flow. Service context characteristics include: i. Service profiles; ii. Service resources, iii. Service qualities (e.g. QoS), iv. Service execution environment characteristics, v. Service configuration characteristics, vi. Service life cycle characteristics.

In a FIN service management system, a service directory that tells one where to access different types of services, should be capable of determining the availability of service context in a dynamically changing network. New tailor-made services can be provided to consumers by dynamically locating sources of different service context.

2.3 DHTs: Overview and Challenges

The solution presented in this paper utilises DHTs whose essential concepts using the Content Addressable Networks (CAN)-DHT as the underlying technique are presented in this Section. The fundamental concepts of different DHT implements are the same. For more detailed information, readers are referred to [10].

The essential element of a DHT is its keyspace. It is represented in a 2D array and is split between the DHT member nodes. Assume that, initially, there is only one node in the FIN. This node, say, node A, owns the entire DHT keyspace (Figure 2a). When the next node (i.e. node B) attempts to join the DHT, the new joining node randomly computes a point in the DHT keyspace. Node A will pass to node B the portion of keyspace that contains the point selected by node B; hence, the original keyspace is split (Figure 2b).

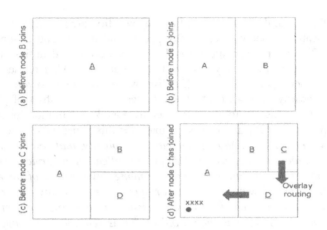

Fig. 2. Example CAN-DHT keyspaces

The keyspace passing process, essentially, means that: i) node A keeps a reference in its record that a portion of its keyspace (which is represented as a 2D array) is now assigned to node B; ii) node A notifies node B about the size of the original 2D array (i.e. the entire key space) and the section of the 2D array that node B has control over. The same applies for other new joining nodes i.e. node D and node C (Figure 2c and Figure 2d). The DHT keyspace ownership for 4 nodes is shown in Figure 2d.

To locate an item using the established DHT, the identifier of the item is hashed. This will map to a point in the DHT keyspace. The node that owns a keyspace portion that covers the point is responsible for holding that item (or holding the address of which the item is located). For example, node C maps an item name to a keyspace point (i.e. point xxxx in Figure 2). This point is covered by the keyspace portion currently owned by node A. However, node C does not see beyond its immediate DHT overlay neighbours (i.e. node B and D). But it knows that the point is "somewhere at the left-hand corner of the DHT keyspace" [11]. It therefore sends a request (i.e. a request for the item of interest) to its immediate overlay neighbour that is in the correct direction, in this case, node D. Node D also knows that the point is somewhere at the left-hand corner of the DHT keyspace; thus, it will pass on the request to node A. Node A can service the request. This decentralise overlay routing feature is an important element of DHTs. It is this feature together with the mapping facility that makes DHTs scalable [10].

We have previously addressed [18] some of the inefficiencies of existing DHTs for wireless and mobile networks. In [27], we have discussed how a large area of wireless network can be covered by multiple DHTs that are bootstrapped to support individual nodes' characteristics and requirements enabling nodes to avoid unnecessary negotiations during the DHT setup and maintenance process. One piece of work that is closely related to the OMB protocol is the RDFPeers [28] that focuses on developing a distributed repository p2p system. It stores triples at three locations in an addressable network, and provides guarantee to quires should the triple exists. Our work in contrast focuses on reducing the need of extended negotiation for setting up the directory service for which a number of challenging issues need to be addressed.

A service directory is capable of collecting information on service availability in FINs, and disseminating the collected information to consumers. Assuming FIN services are pre-defined, perhaps the simplest solution would be to pre-appoint a node (or a set of nodes) in the network to collect and disseminate network-wide service availability information (similar to the idea of having one receptionist which redirects queries in an office). However, such system would be centralised and static, which would not suit the decentralised and dynamic nature of FINs. A challenging approach leads to the investigation of techniques for continuously and dynamically selection of a set of nodes, to act as service directories. These nodes should be capable of keeping track of the real-time availability status of different service context in the network.

The concept of having nodes in the network to carry out management-oriented tasks is similar to the SuperPeer concept in P2P networking [29][30][31], that a subset of peers – that are considered as more capable of carrying certain tasks (such as those with more power, more processing power, etc.) – are dynamically selected or elected to take up certain managerial responsibilities in the network. A set of nodes is preferred because this arrangement is more distributed and more robust: should one node fail, others are there to "backup". SuperPeer election generally requires peers to compete against each other in order to determine the most capable peers in the network.

In rapidly changing network environments with relatively limited-bandwidth, dynamic negotiations for SuperPeer election, and subsequently re-election are not desirable due to the increased overhead they present. The negotiation overhead is dependent on the number of participating nodes (i.e. the more nodes negotiating at one time, the more overhead). It also depends on node mobility (i.e. re-election takes place when nodes move in and out). Thus, high node mobility would, potentially, result in frequent SuperPeer re-election. More importantly, SuperPeer re-election may result in a loop: negotiation → SuperPeer elected → new node joins → re-negotiation.

3 Rlay Management Backbone (OMB)

This section describes fundamental concepts of our solution, the OMB protocol.

3.1 System Overview

Our solution uses DHTs to determine which network nodes become service directories. These nodes are the OMB nodes. An OMB node is responsible for locating a particular type of service context, and disseminating the information to others.

For example in Figure 3a, node OMB_A locates where the requested movie files is, and node OMB_B locates the QoS-controller(s) in the network. These nodes provide the information to support the implementation of the end-user's service. These OMB nodes, together with the node where the end-user resides, the node where the movie file is located, and the node where the QoS-controller is located, creates a service-specific overlay, i.e. a QoS-guaranteed movie-delivery-overlay, to serve the end-user's special needs. The challenge is to dynamically select a set of nodes to become the OMB nodes for different types of service context in the networks, and to re-select the OMB nodes if the selected nodes fail (i.e. when their power runs out, move out of

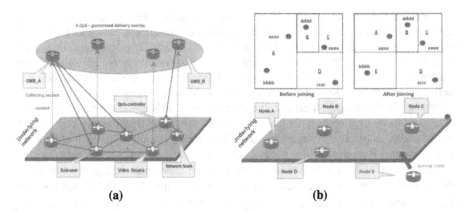

Fig. 3. (a) OMB example in a FIN, (b) Example DHT keyspace ownership

range, etc.). The identities of these selected nodes must also be made known to all other nodes in the network, without additional overhead to suit the limited-bandwidth environment of FINs.

3.2 The OMB Protocol

Our approach towards selecting which node to become which service context locator, i.e. an OMB node that collects information of a particular type of service, is based on a mapping of service names using the DHT protocol. For example, if a DHT uses SHA-256, we will hash the name of the service using SHA-256, which will return a 256-bit keyspace identifier (Figure 4).

The DHT member node that owns the keyspace portion also contains the corresponding keyspace identifiers. This node will become the OMB node responsible for those particular types of service context. Figure 3b for example shows a simple example DHT keyspace ownership in an FIN. Assuming there are initially four nodes in the network, each owns a portion of the DHT keyspace. The keyspace identifiers aaaa and bbbb are within the keyspace portion of node A, thus node A becomes the OMB node for SERVICE_01 and SERVICE_02. This means node A becomes responsible for collecting availability information of movies and QoS-controllers in the network. Similarly, node D owns point cccc, so node D is the OMB node for SERVICE_03, and so on. If node A wants to know which node is the OMB node for SERVICE_03,

```
SERVICE_01 (locate movies):
SHA-256(SERVICE_01) → aaaa
SERVICE_02 (locate QoS-controllers):
SHA-256(SERVICE_02) → bbbb
SERVICE_03 (...):
SHA-256(SERVICE_03) → cccc
```

Fig. 4. Mappings between service names and DHT keyspace identifiers

it maps the name of SERVICE_03 to the corresponding DHT keyspace identifier, i.e. cccc (Figure 3b). Then, by DHT overlay routing, it will (indirectly) route its request to node D, which is the OMB node for SERVICE_03. The advantage of this arrangement is obvious – without any form of (real-time) negotiation, we have achieved two objectives: to dynamically assign service context collection tasks to nodes, and to dynamically disseminate the information on "which node knows what" to others.

3.3 Addressing Node Mobility and Heterogeneity

To illustrate how our system addresses node mobility, assuming a node now joins the DHT (i.e. node E in Figure 3b). When it joins the DHT, it obtains a portion of the DHT keyspace from existing members of the DHT, using the standard/revised DHT protocols (explained in section 2.3). Assuming that it has obtained its keyspace portion from node A, it now owns the keyspace identifier bbbb (Figure 3b). Thus, we say that, node A has "transferred" its responsibility (of SERVICE_02) to node E. This is an importantly feature in our system – it enables balanced loading: the DHT joining process requires random keyspace partitioning; thus, statistically, keyspace ownership is balanced between all DHT nodes. Hence, the OMB load across all nodes in the DHT is also balanced. This enables the OMB protocol to be completely decentralised i.e. no one node is permanently responsible for collecting one type of service context. Also, when new nodes join, tasks are automatically transferred to the new joining node, which enables balanced loading in the network. Also note that, no other nodes in the network needed to be explicitly notified of the recent transferral of responsibility between node A and node E (in contrast to SuperPeer approaches where the identities of new SuperPeers must be explicitly published to peers in the network).

Now, suppose an end-user that resides on node C wants to know which node is responsible for SERVICE_02. Originally, before node E joins the network, node A is responsible for SERVICE_02. When node C maps the service name to keyspace identifiers (i.e. bbbb), it will route its request through DHT overlay routing. For example, it will send its request to node D. Because node D is an immediate overlay neighbour to node E, according to the DHT overlay routing, it knows that node E is likely to be responsible for SERVICE_02 [11]. Hence, node D will pass on the request to node E, which will service node C's request accordingly.

Note that, so far, the discussion assumes that all nodes are capable of carrying out the service context collection tasks that they are assigned to be responsible for. However, in reality, nodes are heterogeneous, they have different features and capabilities. Thus, not all nodes are capable of doing so.

The OMB protocol addresses this heterogeneity issue in the network by requiring the overlay neighbouring nodes to an OMB node (i.e. the original OMB node) to carry out the same service context collection task. These nodes are known as the deputy OMB nodes.

For example in Figure 5a, suppose the original OMB node is expected to be responsible for a particular type of service context. The nodes that own keyspace portions immediate neighbouring to the keyspace portion of the original OMB node (i.e. the ones marked with a hexagon) should carry out the same service context collection task as the original OMB node. These deputy nodes are useful because they act as

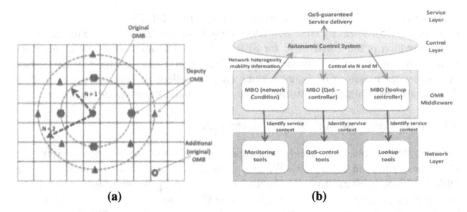

Fig. 5. (a) Example original, deputy, and additional OMB nodes in the DHT; (b) FIN control space and network services

the backups when: 1) the original OMB node is not capable of carrying out its task (e.g. it has little processing power); 2) the original OMB node is no longer capable of carrying out its task (e.g. it runs out of power); 3) the network is heterogeneous i.e. not all deputy nodes are capable of carrying out their tasks; thus a set of deputy nodes are selected so that they can "backup" the original OMB node.

If any of the OMB nodes become incapable, but they are queried by an end-user, the node will query its immediate overlay neighbours (which host the deputy OMB nodes) for the service context of interest. The incapable node also updates its cache with the service context obtained from its neighbours, and responds to the end-user as if it was the source of the result. Optionally, the incapable node or its deputy may also inform the end-user or an autonomic manager through its response that it is in fact an incapable node, and refer the end-user to one of its capable neighbours so that next time such entity can avoid contacting the incapable node.

Generally speaking, the larger the network, or the more heterogeneous the network, more deputy nodes would be needed. Also, if routing locality were optimised, that the overlay neighbourhood maps to physical network neighbourhood, the deputy nodes would tend to be physically near to each other, which would result in uneven load balancing. Thus, we introduce two factors, known as the neighbourhood scale N, and the network scale M, to control the scale of deployment of the OMB protocol.

The factor N determines the radius of deployment of the OMB protocol. For example, in Figure 5a, the radius of deployment is set to 1 and 2 respectively. If N=1, the immediate overlay neighbours to the original OMB node become the deputy OMB nodes (i.e. marked with a hexagon). If N=2, the immediate overlay neighbours to those deputy OMB nodes also become the deputy OMB nodes (i.e. marked with a triangle).

We have discussed that if routing locality is optimised, the deputy nodes tend to locate in nearby neighbourhood, which may result in uneven loading in the network. The M factor is designed to optimise the protocol when uneven loading happens due to optimised routing locality. M=1 when there is only one original OMB node (i.e. the one marked with a dark circle); M=2 when there is an additional (original) OMB node (i.e. the one marked with a hollow circle), and so on. The additional (original) OMB node is determined using a similar approach to the mapping logic as discussed in an earlier section, but by multiple hashing (Figure 6). Multiple hashing means:

1) Hash the service name (i.e. SERVICE_01) with, say, SHA-256, which gives a 256-bit keyspace identifier (#1). The node, which owns a keyspace portion of the DHT that covers this point, is the original OMB node.

2) If M=2, hash the result of step 1 (which was a 256-bit keyspace identifier) using SHA-256, which gives a new 256-bit keyspace identifier (#2). This new identifier refers to another keyspace point in the DHT keyspace (Figure 5a). The node that owns a keyspace portion of the DHT that covers this new point is the additional (original) OMB node.

When M=1:
SHA-256(SERVICE_01) → keyspace point of the original OMB node (#1)
When M=2:
SHA-256(SERVICE_01) → keyspace point of the original OMB node (#1)
SHA-256(SHA-256(SERVICE_01)) → keyspace point of the additional (original) OMB node (#2)

Fig. 6. Multiple hashing

N and M may be used together to control the scale of deployment of the OMB protocol. The values for N and M are determined by the size of the network, and also the level of heterogeneity and mobility of the network (i.e. the failure rate). The level of heterogeneity and mobility are specific to the current conditions of the network, which means they are some form of service context. Thus, they are provided by some network condition monitoring services that are identified and located by OMB nodes. This means that, when a node joins the network, it queries the OMB node that is responsible for locating the network monitoring tools, and obtains the necessary information on N and M.

Figure 5b presents the design of the FIN control space, which utilises available service context in the networks to implement tailor-made end-user services. The OMB node, that is responsible for locating network monitoring tools, provides access to network heterogeneity and mobility information to the FIN (the information on where the monitoring tools are currently located in the network). In turn, the FIN control space uses this information to control the size of deployment of OMB nodes in the network (via N and M).

4 Evaluation

This section evaluates the OMB protocol in terms of scalability, efficiency and robustness. Key OMB features are analysed as compared with other approaches that generally require dynamic negotiation (i.e. SuperPeer [10], RDFPeers [28]). The evaluation software was written in Java and run on a Linux box with an Intel Core2

CPU (1.83GHz) and 1G RAM. Our program essentially contains a 2D array representing a 2D CAN DHT keyspace, which are recursively allocated to joining peers.

4.1 Scalability Advantage of the OMB Protocol

We first compare how many messages would need to be exchanged in order identify the OMB node responsible for collecting information on the availability of a specific type of service context. In the SuperPeer approach, this would be to determine the responsible SuperPeer. We assume that the most suitable SuperPeer is the one with the most processing power. We used broadcast as the mechanism for negotiation in the SuperPeer approach [31][32].

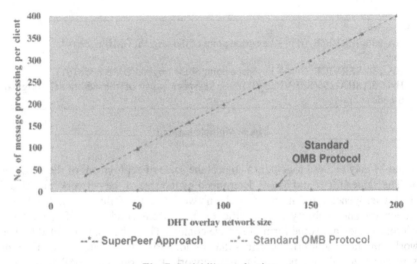

Fig. 7. Scalability evaluation

From the results shown in Figure 7 the SuperPeer approach does not scale due to the number of messages needed to be exchange. Negotiation involves the use of a shared medium (i.e. broadcast), and the negotiation traffic would depend on the size of the entire network. The larger the network, the heavier the overhead. Note that if a new node joins, the same process would have to be repeated. On the other hand, the OMB protocol is much more scalable, dis-regard of the network size. This is achieved through the utilisation of the underlying DHT in the network. As for the storage requirements, a node needs only to maintain a keyspace map, and a list of its immediate physical neighbours. The latter is limited to the ad-hoc range of the device (e.g. a few nodes at most); as for the keyspace maintenance, the node only needs to maintain a list of its virtual neighbours. The degree of this scale of maintenance depends on how evenly fragmented the keyspace is: statistically, load balancing can be assumed in DHT (i.e. every node has equal chance to obtain any portion of the keyspace). Thus, we can safely assume that the keyspace would be divided evenly in the long term; hence, the number of virtual neighbours needed to be maintained by one node is limited.

4.2 Efficiency Advantage

Search efficiency is optimised in DHTs, in the sense that overlay hop count is limited. Standard DHTs do not optimise routing locality meaning that the overlay routing does not map with the underlying physical routing. Our previous work has designed a protocol that optimises DHT routing locality [18][27]. By utilising the underlying DHT in the OMB protocol, search efficiency to locate a particular OMB node is enhanced, too.

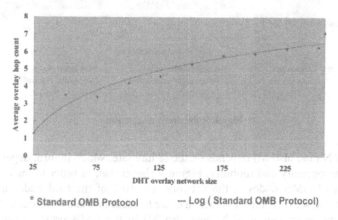

Fig. 8. Efficiency evaluation

The efficiency of the OMB protocol (N=0, hence only one OMB node per service context type) is evaluated by determining the average number of overlay hops needed by a randomly selected end-user node (which is also an overlay member) to reach a particular type of OMB node in the overlay, in networks of different sizes. We assume all nodes in the network are 100% capable of hosting any type of OMB node i.e. node failure rate=0% (see later for evaluation on robustness of OMB node). By setting only one OMB node per type in the network, the average hop count is most likely to be higher.

Figure 8 shows how the overlay hop count varies in overlay networks of different sizes. The OMB protocol is efficient because there are only a few overlay hops in between an OMB node and the end-user (~6 overlay hops for a 225-node network). We have discussed that our protocol is applicable when routing locality is optimised, by having additional (original) OMB nodes in the network. The slope of the curve gradually decreases as the size of network increases. Thus, the effect of a network with an increasing size has limited impact on the search efficiency of the OMB protocol.

4.3 Robustness Evaluation

Robustness (when a failed node is backup by others) evaluation is achieved by adjusting the values of N and M to maintain a certain number of active OMB nodes in the network. We set M=1, so that there is only one original OMB in the network. This OMB node may fail, so we adjust the value of N to increase robustness, which increases the number of deputy OMB nodes in the network. We have discussed that

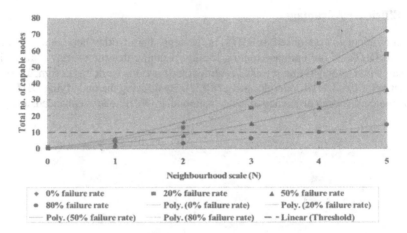

Fig. 9. Robustness evaluation

the value of N (and also M) depends on the failure rate, which in turn, depends on the network heterogeneity and mobility. Figure 9 shows that, in order to maintain a certain number of OMB nodes in the network (i.e. 10% of the total nodes in the network), N can be set to different values in order to accommodate different failure rates. Therefore, the provisioning of N (and also M) in the OMB protocol provides the necessary facility to adjust the level of robustness.

The OMB protocol is designed for scalability, efficiency and robustness. The identities of the OMB nodes are determined and disseminated dynamically without any form of dynamic negotiation: the underlying DHT enables any users to efficiently locate which node is responsible for which type of service context. Also, consumers or autonomic managers may access service availability information via the original, deputy, and additional OMB nodes in the network, which means single point of failure is avoided. The end-user's request routes its way through the DHT to the (original) OMB node via DHT overlay routing. Thus, the request is intercepted and serviced by the first intercepting OMB node. This means that, the system is decentralised. Also, efficiency is enhanced because an end-user's request may be serviced by the nearest OMB node.

The load-balancing feature of the OMB protocol makes OMB more scalable and efficient: no one node in the network is responsible for collecting one type of service context. In fact, the entire system is distributed, that when new nodes join, responsibilities may be transferred to these nodes. Similarly, if an OMB node becomes an incapable node, its assigned responsibilities are automatically transferred to the backup nodes. All these are made possible without any form of dynamic negotiation between nodes.

5 Conclusions and Further Work

The key concept of Future Internet Network (FIN) is to develop a common control space, which enables service sharing across heterogeneous end-user devices through wired and wireless channels. In order to utilise service deployment in FINs, there is a need for a system that can dynamically determine the availability of different types of service context in the network. This implies that, some service directories, which indicate which service is available where, are needed in FINs. This service directory should have a self-organising mechanism that would efficiently and automatically determine a set of nodes in the network to carry out dedicated service context tasks. Existing similar approaches, such as the SuperPeer approaches, use real-time negotiations to assign tasks to the most suitable nodes in the network. However, due to node mobility, the negotiation process may result in a loop. Also, the higher the level of dynamicity in the network, the more frequent the negotiation process may take place. Since negotiations are usually conducted through broadcast or multicast, frequent negotiation means frequent broadcast or multicast. Frequent use of a shared medium, particularly in bandwidth-limited environment, should be avoided.

This paper presented the OMB protocol, which enables automatic and self-organising service context task assignations in FINs. No dynamic negotiation is needed between peers even when the network has a high mobility. The OMB protocol features load balancing, by evenly distributing service context tasks to peers in the network through the utilisation of the underlying DHT in FINs. Our solution is completely decentralised and self-organised, and it is designed to be efficient and scalable. Enhanced robustness of the protocol is achieved by adjusting the values of N and M respectively, which controls the number of active OMB nodes in the network.

Future work includes: i. use of OMBs for different network management applications; ii. applying and using the OMB protocol for management of virtual networks; iii. quantification of the level of mobility/or network topology change; iii. assessing the impact of energy usage in the OMB selection; iv. synchronisation of deputies with the original nodes; v. defining a scalable and efficient mechanism for all nodes within the FIN control space to participate in request for tailored consumers' service proposals, assuming participant nodes have their own interests of association, service provisioning constraints, level of commitment and their own business objectives. The goal for this critical mechanism is to quickly converge towards an acceptable solution for the provisioning of the target service; vi. An Autonomic Network Programming Interface (ANPI) dedicated to autonomic services deployment in the networks is currently under development. It will be based on the OMB protocol to efficiently access to large decentralized service repositories.

Acknowledgments

Part of this work was undertaken in the context of the Autonomic Internet project [17] and Ambient Networks project [5], which are partially financed by the EU.

References

[1] Bassi, A., Denazis, S., Galis, A., Fahy, C., Serrano, M., Serrat, J.: Autonomic Internet: A Perspective for Future Internet Services Based on Autonomic Principles. In: IEEE 3rd Intl. Week on Management of Networks and Services Manweek 2007 / MACE 2007 2nd IEEE International Workshop on Modelling Autonomic Communications Environments, San José, California, USA, October 29 – November 2 (2007)

[2]   Future Internet Design (FIND) Program, http://www.nets-find.net/
[3]   Global Environment for Network Innovation (GENI) Program,
      http://www.geni.net/
[4]   Future Internet Assembly (FIA)/ FIRE program, http://www.fi-bled.eu/
      http://cordis.europa.eu/fp7/ict/fire/home_en.html
[5]   Ambient Networks (ANs) Project, http://www.ambient-networks.org
[6]   Mobile Ad-hoc NETworks (MANETs),
      http://www.ietf.org/html.charters/manet-charter.html
[7]   Gnutella development forum, the gnutella v0.6 protocol,
      http://groups.yahoo.com/group/thegdf/files/
[8]   Bittorrent, http://bitconjurer.org/BitTorrent/
[9]   Clarke, I., Sandberg, O., Wiley, B., Hong, T.W.: Freenet: A distributed anonymous in-
      formation storage and retrieval system. Freenet White Paper (1999)
[10] Lua, E., Crowcroft, J., Pias, M., Sharma, R., Lim, S.: A Survey and Comparison of Peer-
      to-Peer Overlay Network Schemes. In: IEEE Communications Survey and Tutorial
      (March 2004)
[11] Ratnasamy, S., Francis, P., Handley, M., Karp, R., Shenker, S.: A Scalable Content-
      Addressable Network. In: ACM conference on Applications, technologies, architectures,
      and protocols for computer communications (SIGCOMM), pp. 161–172, San Diego, CA,
      USA (August 2001)
[12] Rowstron, D.P.: Pastry: Scalable, distributed object location and routing for large-scale
      peer-to-peer systems. In: Guerraoui, R. (ed.) Middleware 2001. LNCS, vol. 2218, pp.
      329–350. Springer, Heidelberg (2001)
[13] Stoica, I., Morris, R., Karger, D., Kaashoek, M.F., Balakrishnan, H.: Chord: A Scalable
      Peer-to-peer Lookup Service for Internet Applications. In: The ACM conference on Ap-
      plications, technologies, architectures, and protocols for computer communications
      (SIGCOMM), San Diego, USA (August 2001)
[14] Zach, M., Parker, D., Fahy, C., Carroll, R., Lehtihet, E., Georgalas, N., Marin, R., Serrat,
      J., Nielsen.: Towards a framework for network management applications based on peer-
      to-peer paradigms. In: NOMS 2006, Vancouver, Canada (2006)
[15] Booth, D., Haas, H., McCabe, F., Newcomer, E., Champion, M., Ferris, C., Orchard, D.:
      Web Services Architecture. In: W3C Working Group Note, W3C (Febraury 2004)
[16] Fehskens, A.: Monitoring Systems. In: 1st IFIP Integrated Network Management Sympo-
      sium, Boston (May 1989)
[17] Autonomic Internet Project, http://www.ist-autoi.eu
[18] Cheng, L., Ocampo, R., Jean, K., Galis, A., Simon, C., Szabo, R., Kersch, P., Giaffreda,
      R.: Towards Distributed Hash Tables (De)Composition in Ambient Networks. In: State,
      R., van der Meer, S., O'Sullivan, D., Pfeifer, T. (eds.) DSOM 2006. LNCS, vol. 4269, pp.
      258–298. Springer, Heidelberg (2006)
[19] Strassner, J., Agoulmine, N., Lehtihet, E.: FOCALE—A Novel Autonomic Computing
      Architecture, LAACS (2006)
[20] Curran, K., Mulvenna, M., Galis, A., Nugent, C.: Challenges and Research Directions in
      Autonomic Communications. International Journal of Internet Protocol Technology
      (IJIPT) 2(1), 3–17 (2007); SSN (Online): 1743-8217- ISSN (Print):
[21] Schilit, B., Theimer, M.: Disseaminating Active Map Information to Mobile Hosts. IEEE
      Network 8(5), 22–32 (1994)
[22] Brown, M.: Supporting User Mobility. International Federation for Information Process-
      ing (1996)

[23] Schilit, B., Adams, N., Want, R.: Context-Aware Computing Applications. In: The IEEE Computer Society Workshop on Mobile Computing Systems and Applications, pp. 85–90. IEEE, Santa Cruz (1994)

[24] Pascoe, J.: Adding Generic Contextual Capabilities to Wearable Computers. In: The 2nd International Symposium on Wearable Computers, pp. 92–99 (1998)

[25] Dey, A., Salber, D., Abowd, G.: The Context Toolkit: Aiding the Development of Context-Enabled Applications. In: The 1999 ACM Conference on Human Factors in Computer Systems (CHI 1999), pp. 434–441. ACM Press, PA (1999)

[26] Galis, A., De Meer, H., Todd, C.: Flow Context Tags: Concepts and Applications. In: NetCon 2005 Conference, Lannion, France, November 14-18 (2005)

[27] Cheng, L., Jean, K., Ocampo, R., Galis, A., Kersch, P., Szabo, R.: Secure Bootstrapping of Distributed Hash Tables in Dynamic Wireless Networks. In: The IEEE International Conference on Communications (ICC), Glasgow, UK (June 2007)

[28] Cai, M., Frank, M.: RDFPeers: A Scalable Distributed RDF Repository based on a Structured Peer-to-Peer Network. In: 13th Intl. Conf. on World Wide Web, NY, USA, May 17-20 (2004)

[29] Kleis, M., Lua, E., Zhou, X.: Hierarchical Peer-to-Peer Networks using Lightweight SuperPeer Topologies, In: The 10th IEEE Symposium Computers and Communications (ISCC), Cartagena, Spain, pp. 143–148 (June 2005)

[30] Jesi, G., Montresor, A., Babaoglu, O.: Proximity-Aware SuperPeer Overlay Topologies. In: The 2nd IEEE International Workshop on Self-Managed Networks, Systems & Services (SelfMan), Dublin, Ireland (June 2006)

[31] Mizrak, A., Cheung, Y., Kumar, V., Savage, S.: Structured SuperPeers: Leveraging Heterogeneity to Provide Constant-Time Lookup. In: The IEEE Workshop on Internet Applications (WIAPP), San Jose, USA (June 2003)

[32] Adler, M., Kumar, R., Ross, K., Rubenstein, D., Suel, T., Yao, D.: Optimal Peer Selection for P2P Downloading and Streaming. In: The IEEE Infocom, Miami, FL (March 2005)

Achieving Self-management in a Distributed System of Autonomic BUT Social Entities

N. Samaan

School of Information Technology & Engineering (SITE), University of Ottawa
nsamaan@site.uottawa.ca

Abstract. This paper presents a novel self-management model for resource allocation in an autonomic system (AS) comprised of individual, but social, autonomic entities (AEs). Each AE is associated with an interdependent utility function that, not only models its utility over its resource allocations, but also depends on other AEs allocations and, hence, the global AS welfare. Pervious utility-based approaches are limited to representing the AS as a set of independent AEs that aim at self-optimizing their performance unaware of other AEs' behavior. In contrast to these dominant approaches, the proposed scheme efficiently models various social behaviors, such as cooperation, selfishness and competition, among those AEs to dynamically change the overall resource allocations in different scenarios such as in the case of anomalies or varying service demands. These behavior patterns are incorporated into the utility function of each AE which is composed of two components, local and global utilities. The former reflects the AE's utility of its resource consumption while the latter is dependent on the other AEs' consumptions. By controlling these utilities, AEs create a social community where they lend/borrow resources and reward/punish other well/mal- behaving AEs. Experimental results demonstrate that creating such a social AS is more efficient than simplified systems of independent utilities.

Keywords: Autonomic computing; utility functions; interdependent utilities.

1 Introduction

Distributed computing systems, including geographically dispersed networking systems, grid computing environments, and massive data centers, are becoming an integral part of our lives today. These systems uniquely federate and manage heterogeneous resources across multiple domains to provide services for a large number of users. However, as their complexity and size continue to grow exponentially, the management of these systems is becoming a bottleneck, and hence, necessitating the development of efficient self-management solutions. The basic goal of these solutions is to allow any distributed system to continuously monitor its own behavior and to adapt its operations with minimal supervision. Ultimately, the success of these solutions would create what is referred to as an autonomic system (AS) that is capable of self -configuring, -healing, -optimizing and -protecting while optimally achieving high-level objectives [1].

A typical AS may be comprised of a large number of autonomic entities (AEs) that can utilize a set of shared resources (e.g., link bandwidth and queues in autonomic communication systems [2] and CPU and memory in autonomic data centers [3]) to deliver

S. van der Meer, M. Burgess, and S. Denazis (Eds.): MACE 2008, LNCS 5276, pp. 90–101, 2008.

a set of services. The overall performance of the AS emerges from the behavior of its individual AEs which must dynamically relocate available resources among themselves based on current service demands and resource availability. These entities are faced with three main challenges: the highly varying demands of the requesting services, the dynamic availability of the resources, and the threats of resource monopoly by selfish or highly demanding AEs that might be behaving normally or abnormally, for instance, due to external attacks. The first problem has been the focus of intensive research efforts (e.g., [4]) that target the development of efficient models to capture the varying demands of different applications and services. Hence, this paper focuses on the latter two problems which are explained herein. In any AS, AEs share a finite amount of resources, consequently, they must collaborate to optimally allocate these resources to maximize the overall system performance. More precisely, AEs must interact together and cooperate to achieve varying global system goals such as increasing resource usage priorities to critical services, maintaining fair resource allocations and decreasing response times. These goals must be attained during normal operations as well as during external attacks and security threats. For example, an entity attacked by a malicious software that aims at draining system resources must be sensed and eliminated by other entities in order to avoid degrading or even failing the whole system.

Utility-based approaches represent a promising solution to the aforementioned challenges [5, 3]. A utility function can be defined as the mapping of a set of preferences, describing an entity's resource usage, to a real numeric value that reflects the entity's gain expressed in terms of service level attributes (e.g., response time). Hence, the collection of individual entities' utilities can be used to build a model of the entire AS behavior. In turn, by using this model, efficient resource allocations can be found by solving an optimization problem either centrally through a resource broker [6] or in a distributed manner [5]. However, the main limitation of current utility-based approaches is that they work under the assumption that an AS is comprised of a set of independent utility-maximizing AEs, where the resource allocations for one is irrelevant to the utility of the others. Hence, the total AS goal is, in turn, represented as a sum of totally independent goals. This simplified model does not provide incentives for entities to cooperate nor does it allow AEs to eliminate mal-behaving AEs. To further illustrate this problem, consider a selfish AE that sets its utility to be largely bigger than all other AEs. The result is that all other entities will suffer from resource starvation. However, the global utility, reflected by the sum of all utilities, will not be significantly affected due to the dominant utility of that entity.

Cohen [7] has shown that, in complex environments, cooperation becomes more advantageous compared to self-interest alone. Based on this premise, an efficient AS model must be designed with two objectives in mind. The first is to allow each AE to describe its local objectives that target the maximization of its own utility. On the other hand, the second objective of the model is to provide the means for the AEs to interact in order to achieve some desired global objectives where they can share and exchange resources according to the dynamics of the AS. An AE may, for example, lend resources to certain AEs that had collaborated with it in the past and compete for resources with those entities that are behaving selfishly. The proposed self-management model achieves the aforementioned objectives by borrowing concepts from the literature of behavioral economics. In economic models [8], agents do not act as purely selfish individuals but engage in behaviors derived by the satisfaction perceived from the consumption of economic goods by individuals other than the referenced agents. To create this pattern of behavior in ASs, the proposed model allows each AE to express its utility as a function of two components, a local- and a global- utility. The former reflects the individual gains of the AE based on its resource allocations, while the latter is dependent on the other AEs' consumptions. By varying the entity's global utility, different behaviors, such as cooperation, competition and selfishness, create a social community where AEs lend/borrow resources and reward/punish other well/mal- behaving AEs.

The rest of the paper is organized as follows; in Section 2, related work is discussed. Section 3 describes the adopted AS model and provides an analysis of the limitations of independent utilities. The proposed self-management model is presented in Section 4. Illustrative examples and numerical results are provided in Sections 5 and 6, respectively. Finally, Section 7 concludes the paper and discusses future research directions.

2   Related Work

The work presented in this paper is relevant to two strands of research areas in the literature: utility-based self-management and efficient models of complex AS.

2.1   Utility-Based Self-management

Within the Unity project [6], utility functions are used to arbitrate resource allocation among different application environments. This approach was extended in [3] with utility policies that define the desired performance goals in terms of utility functions. Self-management is then achieved by selecting the best system configurations as a result of solving an optimization problem. In a similar manner, utility functions were used in [9] to adapt network configurations. In this approach, the most appropriate policy actions for the current context of the network are selected from a predefined pool of all possible actions to be applied at the network-levels based on their forecasted behavior. Utility functions are also used to compose and update the end-to-end communication paths [10] with the highest service quality. In this approach, an optimization engine takes, as an input, a set of route requirements in terms of service quality, and a weighted graph representing the current capabilities and constraints of each participating network domain and finds the optimal paths by solving a multi-constrained optimal path problem.

The main focus of the aforementioned approaches was addressing the gap between business level objectives and system level configurations. While utility functions were successfully applied to overcome this gap, they do not capture or allow the dynamic behavior of the AS components.

2.2   Advanced Models of Autonomic Systems

The work presented in this paper is also relevant to research efforts that aim at modeling complex behaviors of the autonomic entities. The dominant approaches in this area apply different techniques such as reinforcement learning, biologically inspired solutions, and evolutionary computing theories, to realize varying autonomic behaviors; A sample of these efforts are described herein.

Reinforcement learning is applied in [11] to realize a goal-based approach to policy refinement where low-level actions are selected to satisfy a high-level goal using inference and concepts of the event-calculus theory. Another approach [12] attaches a description of the system behavior, in terms of resource utilization and its effects on service levels, to each specified rule. Behavior implications are used to derive different self-management strategies. Dowling et al. [13] apply concepts of collaborative reinforcement learning to allow agents to collaboratively self-manage their behavior at run-time. Reinforcement learning is achieved through simple positive and negative feedback among agents and is used to learn optimal routing policies. An agent's experience with a non-optimal routing (e.g., congested route) results in exchanging negative feedback messages and, vice versa, a good connection is reflected by an increase in the reward messages. [14]. One limitation of reinforcement learning approaches is the need to maintain a precise model of all exhaustive system states.

Biologically inspired solutions have also been considered for self-management. For example, swarm intelligence concepts are applied to automate the control of network management problems such as load balancing [15] and route construction [16]. The main advantage to such approaches is their extended temporal and spatial scopes and the flexibility in modifying their purposefulness and strategies. Similarly, self-management approaches using evolutionary computing aim at moving or expanding system capabilities for adaptation by learning new or modified strategies. For example, in [17], proxy servers or routers are modeled as bacteria and service requests as food, where each bacterium has an amount of genetic material that codes for the rule set by which it lives. The system then evolves its adaptation through gene migration and random mutation.

In contrast to the aforementioned approaches, the proposed work aims at modeling primary social behaviors among AEs that can be applied to create more complex interactions allowing the AS to dynamically change in response to external effects such as varying service demands or due to security threats.

3 The Autonomic System Model

As shown in Figure 1, the distributed system under consideration is a generic AS $S=\{E_1, E_2, \cdots, E_M\}$ that consists of M logically separated autonomic entities (AEs), $E_i, i = 1, \cdots, M$. Each AE provides a set of services to end users and consumes a set of resources dynamically allocated to it from a shared, finite pool $\mathcal{R} = \{\bar{R}_1, \bar{R}_2, \cdots, \bar{R}_N\}$ of N resources. Kephart et al. [1] provide a popular framework for AEs; Each AE is responsible for monitoring its performance and managing its own internal behavior. Since the resources in any system are finite, one of the main challenges for an AE's self-management process is to regulate its own resource usage in order to achieve its own goals as well as that of the entire AS. As described earlier, utility-based approaches represent a popular stream of solutions to the above problem. In these approaches, each AE E_i, has its own utility function $u_i(R_i)$, that controls its behavior. This function describes the AE utility or gain as a function of its allocated resources represented by

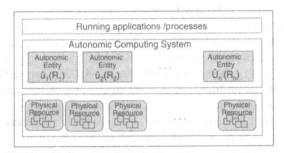

Fig. 1. A schematic description of an autonomic system (AS)

the N-dimensional vector $R_i = \{r_{i1}, r_{i2}, \cdots, r_{iN}\}$. Here, $r_{ij} \in [0,1]$ represents the amount of $\bar{R}_j$ allocated to E_i, such that

$$\sum_{i=1}^{M} r_{ij} \leq \bar{R}_j, \forall j = 1, \cdots, N \tag{1}$$

In this paper, we consider the general case where a resource $\bar{R}_j$ can be shared among several AEs. It is worth noting that this model can be reduced to represent the special case of unshared resources by restricting the values of r_{ij} to be in the set $\{0,1\}$.

One example of the described AS is an autonomic communication system that is comprised of N links and M entities each dedicated to servicing one or more user flows. Another example is an autonomic data center (e.g., [3]) that contains N dedicated data servers servicing M autonomous application environments.

3.1   Limitations of Independent Utility-Based Self-management Schemes

The dominant utility-based approaches to self-management work under the assumption that $u_i(R_i)$ is only dependent on R_i and is independent of the other AE's consumptions or utilities. This approach is attractive due to its simplicity where the total AS utility U_S from a given resource allocation described by the matrix $R_S = (R_1 \; R_2 \cdots R_M)^T = (r_{ij})_{i,j}$ can be directly described as the sum of all the utilities, i.e.,

$$U_S(R_S) = \sum_{i=1}^{M} u_i(R_i) \tag{2}$$

The optimal resource allocation for S is then obtained by solving an optimization problem [3] to find R^* such that:

$$R^* = \arg\max_{R_S} \sum_{i=1}^{M} u_i(R_i) \quad \text{s.t} \quad \sum_{i} r_{ij} = \bar{R}_j \quad \forall j = 1, \cdots, N \tag{3}$$

The problem of the utility in (2) is that it attempts to optimize a global objective that is derived from individual AEs' independent goals. While the solution may be optimal to individual entities, it may not necessary yield an optimal utility for the overall AS.

In other words, an optimal utility for individual AEs is not always equivalent to the optimal utility for the overall system [7]. Another limitation is that it lacks the ability to describe the social ties among the entities that may dynamically enhance and evolve the overall AS' behavior. These relationships are also important to increase the overall system tolerance to external effects (e.g., security threats). For example, consider an autonomic communication system servicing a set of flows; if the behavior of a router becomes anomalous (e.g., due to a denial of service attack), obviously, this entity will try to maximize its resource utility (bandwidth in this case) to fulfill its malicious tasks. Based on the constraints in (3), an increase in one AE's resource usage will result in a decrease in other AEs allocations, starving the other AEs and eventually the system may fail. However, no significant decrease in the overall utility (as described by (3)) will be apparent. On the contrary, in an AS, it is expected that other AEs can detect an anomalous AE and cooperate to reduce its resources utilization. Now, consider another scenario, where an autonomic router is tasked with routing a high priority and time critical flow that has a sudden but temporary increase in bandwidth needs, it would be desirable that all neighboring autonomic routers and those that share paths with the flow would cooperate, sacrificing their resource utilities, for a short period of time, but only for this flow. Again, the model described by (2) fails to achieve this form of cooperation.

In the following section, a new model is presented to overcome the aforementioned limitations. By borrowing concepts of interdependent utilities [8] from the field of social economics, novel and efficient AEs' utilities that can capture the dynamics of the above scenarios are represented.

4 Proposed Social Self-management Scheme

In this section, a novel model of a social AS that is comprised of interdependent AEs is proposed. The model satisfies two main characteristics; the first is that each AE is derived by the objective of maximizing its own self-interests. The second characteristic is that each AE can influence the resource allocations of other AEs, and hence, creating social interactions among those AEs with the objective of maximizing the overall system welfare. These two characteristics are realized by adopting concepts of interdependent utilities used in social economics [8].

As in the independent utility case (e.g., [3]), each AE, E_i, has its own utility $u_i(R_i)$ on its own resource consumption, therein referred to as the *local utility*. However, E_i has another *global utility*, $u_{\curvearrowright i}(.)$, that describes its interest in resources allocated to other AEs. Each AE will be responsible for adapting its interactions with other entities by adjusting these two utilities. The new total utility of E_i, $\hat{u}_i(R_i)$ is a function of both the local and global utilities, i.e.,

$$\hat{u}_i(.) = f(u_i(R_i), u_{\curvearrowright i}(.))$$
$$u_{\curvearrowright i}(.) = f(f_{i1}(\hat{u}_1(R_1)), \cdots ,$$
$$f_{ii-1}(\hat{u}_{i-1}(R_{i-1})), f_{ii+1}(\hat{u}_{i+1}(R_{i+1})), \cdots , f_{iM}(\hat{u}_M(R_M))) \quad (4)$$

One can interpret the global utility, $u_{\curvearrowright i}$, as a summarization of each AE's social concerns about other AEs, where each component, f_{ij} reflects concern of E_i towards E_j

for $i \neq j$. This can include the desire to sacrifice resources for some AEs, to punish selfish entities by acquiring their resources or to act independently of other entities. Hence, achieving the social behaviors discussed in Section 2.

More precisely, E_i is said to be cooperative with E_j when the function $\hat{u}_i$ is increasing in $u_j(R_j)$. This cooperative behavior is viable when an AE requires assistance from other AEs to achieve its goals or during cases of failure of a required resource. On the other hand, an E_i is said to be punishing, or hindering to E_j when $\hat{u}_i$ is decreasing in $u_j(R_j)$. Punishment behavior is needed to limit resource utilization of malicious entities or to discourage uncooperative behavior of other entities. Finally, selfish behavior by all entities reduces the system to the case of independent utilities.

Using the interdependent utilities in (4), the new AS utility can be described as:

$$U_S = \sum_{i=1}^{M} \hat{u}_i(.) = \sum_{i=1}^{M} f(u_i(R_i), u_{\sim i}(.)), \quad \text{s.t} \quad \sum_i r_{ij} = \bar{R}_j \quad \forall j = 1, \cdots, N \quad (5)$$

Similar to the model in (3), the optimal resource allocation, R^*, that maximizes the overall utility $U_S(R^*)$ can be found by solving an optimization problem. It is clear that the solution-sets of (3) and (5) are usually not identical. The main advantage of the AS model described in (5) is that such interdependent utilities allow for a more dynamic and efficient resource allocation among the AEs. In the following section, an analysis of different AE behavior patterns is provided.

4.1 Modeling the Various Behavior Patterns

An AE may exhibit different forms of social behaviors towards another AE by modifying its global utility $u_{\sim i}(.)$ as follows:

- **Cooperative behavior:** E_i is said to be cooperative with E_j if E_i may reduce (or lend) its resource allocations to redistribute scare resources to E_j when E_j is capable of maximizing the overall AS utility. The social welfare of the AS, in this case, improves only if the beneficiary E_j's benefit outweighs the benefactor E_i's cost, i.e., if $\hat{u}_i(R_i^* - R_{ij}) < \hat{u}_i(R_j^* + R_{ij})$, where R_{ij} is the amount of transferred resources. Hence, when the utility of one is increased, the overall performance of the AS will also increase. This relationship can be modeled by the sample functions $f_{ij}(u_j)$ in Figure 2(a).
- **Punishment behavior:** E_i is said to be punishing E_j if it hinders its resource consumption. In this case, E_i is redistributing resources allocated to E_j among other AEs. This relationship can be modeled by the graphs in Figures 2(b). Such behavior can be applied to punish uncooperative or mal-behaving AEs. In this case, entities can collaborate against a malicious AE.
- **Selfish behavior:** An AE, E_i, is said to be of self-interest or selfish towards E_j if its utility is irrelevant of the resources allocated to E_j; in this case $f_{ij}(u_j) = 0$.
- **Mixed behavior:** An AE E_i's behavior towards E_j may be dependent on the amount of resources currently allocated to both of these entities. For example, E_i may be cooperative with E_j as long as the allocated resources for (or the utility of) the latter do not exceed that of E_i. For example, E_i may only cooperate with E_j if its cooperation minimizes the difference $(u_i(R_i) - u_j(R_j))$, but maintains its positive sign. Figure 2(c), provides some sample functions to model this behavior.

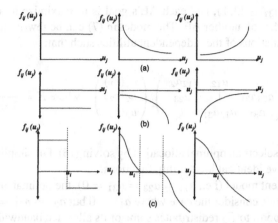

Fig. 2. Sample functions modeling different patterns of E_i behavior towards E_j

5 Illustrative Examples: Linearly Interdependent Entities

To maintain lucidity in presenting the proposed model, we consider simple interdependent AS model comprised of AEs with linearly additive relationships, i.e., the total utility function of each AE, E_i, can be described as:

$$\hat{u}_i(R_i) = u_i(R_i) + \sum_{j \neq i} a_{ij} \hat{u}_j(R_j) \quad i = 1, \cdots, M \qquad (6)$$

where a_{ij} is a real number that reflects E_i's well to cooperate with or hinder E_j. When $a_{ij} > 0$ then E_i is cooperating with E_j and, vice versa, when $a_{ij} < 0$, E_i is uncooperative with E_j. Moreover, when $a_{ij} > 0$ and $a_{ji} > 0$, then E_i and E_j are mutually supportive. Conversely, when $a_{ij} < 0$ and $a_{ji} < 0$, E_i and E_j are mutually conflicting. Finally, if $a_{ij} = 0$ then E_j is irrelevant to E_i.

The examples provided in the following sections illustrate how the model represented by (6) can be applied to represent different social interactions among AEs.

5.1 Example 1: Modeling Cooperative Behaviors

Consider the autonomic communication system presented in Figure 3. The system is comprised of three AEs, E_1, E_2 and E_3, each servicing flows of a single user. The AEs are competing over the available bandwidth R of the bottleneck link between E_4 and E_5 and adjust their transmission rates according to their allocations $R^* = (r_1^*, r_2^*, r_3^*)$ which are determined by the resource arbitrator E_4 according to their total utilities. The total utilities are described as follows:

$$\hat{u}_1(.) = u_1(r_1) + a_{12}\hat{u}_2(.) \qquad (7)$$
$$\hat{u}_2(.) = u_2(r_2) + a_{23}\hat{u}_3(.)$$
$$\hat{u}_3(.) = u_3(r_3) + a_{31}\hat{u}_1(.)$$

Where $a_{12}, a_{12}, a_{31} \in [0, 1)$, i.e., each AE's goal is to maximize its own bandwidth utility as well as that of another AE. The model in (7) can be rewritten to describe the total utilities as functions of the independent utilities such that:

$$
\begin{pmatrix} \hat{u}_1(.) \\ \hat{u}_2(.) \\ \hat{u}_3(.) \end{pmatrix} = K \begin{pmatrix} 1 & a_{12} & a_{12}a_{23} \\ a_{23}a_{31} & 1 & a_{23} \\ a_{31} & a_{12}a_{31} & 1 \end{pmatrix} \begin{pmatrix} u_1(r_1) \\ u_2(r_2) \\ u_3(r_3) \end{pmatrix}, \text{ where } K = \frac{1}{1 - a_{12}a_{23}a_{31}} \tag{8}
$$

The arbitrator E_4 selects an optimal allocation by solving (5). For simplicity, we assume that all entities have identical local utility functions.

In an independent model (i.e., $a_{11} = a_{23} = a_{31} = 0$), the optimal allocations are $\frac{R}{3}$ for each entity. Now, consider the case where $a_{12} > 0$ but $a_{23} = a_{31} = 0$, from (8) it is clear that E_1's support to E_2 redistributes some of its allocated bandwidth such that the new optimal allocation for E_2 increases by a factor of a_{12} while reducing allocations to both E_1 and E_3. Now, if $a_{12} > 0, a_{23} > 0$ but $a_{31} = 0$, the support provided to E_2 is partially transferred to E_3, increasing the allocations to E_3 by a factor of $a_{12}a_{23} + a_a{23}$. Finally, when $a_{12} > 0, a_{23} > 0$ and $a_{31} > 0$, the bandwidth is redistributed in a manner that is dependent on the strength of the cooperation of each entity. In other words, by negotiating a_{12}, a_{23} and a_{31}, E_1, E_2 and E_3 control their own resource usage and that of the others. Furthermore, when all are equally cooperative, the system becomes equivalent to that of the independent case.

5.2   Example2: Modeling Punishment Behavior

Now, consider the same configuration of Figure 3, but with mutual cooperation between E_1 and E_2 while punishing E_3, such that:

$$
\begin{aligned}
\hat{u}_1(.) &= u_1(r_1) + (a_{12}\hat{u}_2(.) - a_{13}\hat{u}_2(.)) \\
\hat{u}_2(.) &= u_2(r_2) + (a_{21}\hat{u}_1(.) - a_{23}\hat{u}_3(.)) \\
\hat{u}_3(.) &= u_3(r_3)
\end{aligned} \tag{9}
$$

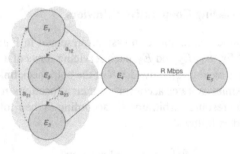

Fig. 3. A sample autonomic communication system

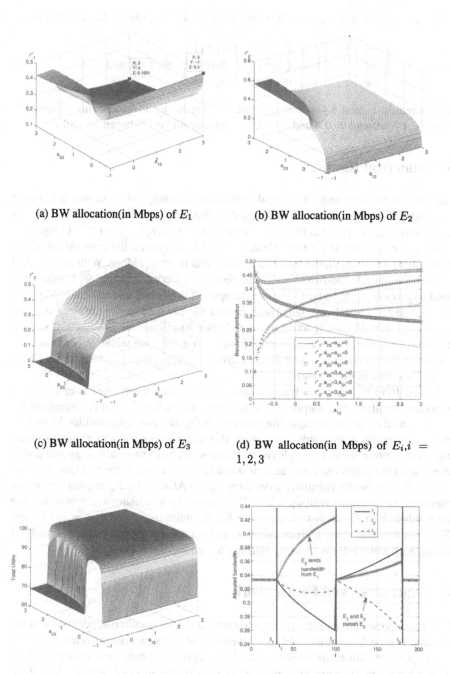

(a) BW allocation(in Mbps) of E_1

(b) BW allocation(in Mbps) of E_2

(c) BW allocation(in Mbps) of E_3

(d) BW allocation(in Mbps) of $E_i, i = 1, 2, 3$

(e) Total Utility

(f) Social behaviors among AEs

Fig. 4. Performance of the social AS model described in (7)

Let $a_{12}=a_{21}= a$ and $a_{13}=a_{23}= b$, where $a, b \in [0, 1)$, then (9) can be rewritten as:

$$
\begin{pmatrix} \hat{u}_1(.) \\ \hat{u}_2(.) \\ \hat{u}_3(.) \end{pmatrix} = \begin{pmatrix} \frac{1}{K} & \frac{a}{K} & \frac{b}{a-1} \\ \frac{a}{K} & \frac{1}{K} & \frac{b}{a-1} \\ 0 & 0 & 1 \end{pmatrix} \begin{pmatrix} u_1(r_1) \\ u_2(r_2) \\ u_3(r_3) \end{pmatrix}, \text{ where } K = 1 - a^2 \qquad (10)
$$

As b increases, E_1 and E_2 cooperate to punish E_3 reducing its resource allocations. For example, by setting $b = 0.5$ and $a = 0$, R is equally divided between E_1 and E_2.

6 Numerical Results

This section provides some numerical results for the configuration shown in Figure 3 when adopting the interdependent model described in (7). The local utility, $u_i(r_i)$ of each entity, E_i, $i = 1, 2, 3$ is set to the convex function $u_i(r_i) = 1 - e^{-br_i}$ to represent utilities of elastic traffic sources. Here, $b = 9.2$ is a constant the controls the shape of the utility function. R, the bottleneck bandwidth is set to 1Mbps. With independent utilities, the optimal bandwidth allocation remains at a constant value $\frac{R}{3}$. On the other hand, Figures 4(a), (b) and (c) illustrate the optimal bandwidth allocations, in Mpbs, to E_1, E_2 and E_3, respectively, when both E_1 and E_2 vary their global utilities, such that $a_{12}, a_{21} \in (-1,3)$-$\{1\}$, while fixing $a_{31} = 0$. Figure 4(d) illustrates the effects of varying the behavior of E_1 in two cases: when the two other entities are selfish ($a_{23} = a_{31} = 0$) and when E_2 is cooperative and E_3 is selfish (a_{23}=3, a_{31}=0). The total utility of the system is shown in Figure 4(e).

Figure 4(f) illustrates the dynamic interactions among the entities over four time intervals. For illustrative purposes, it is assumed that each entity can communicate directly with other entities to request/respond to lending/borrowing bandwidth. Moreover, each entity randomly responds to a request. It is worth noting that a more sophisticated negotiation protocol can be employed or changes can be dynamically triggered due to monitored events, this issue will be considered in future work. At the first time interval, $t < t_1$, the bandwidth is equally shared among the AEs. At t_1, E_2 requests the cooperation of the two other entities, where E_1 responds by increasing a_{12}, hence, lending the bandwidth to E_2 up to $t = t_2$, while E_3 maintains $a_{31} = 0$. At $t = t_2$, E_1 and E_2 respond by punishing E_3 increasing a_{12} and decreasing a_{23} respectively. Finally, at $t = t_3$, each entity returns to acting selfishly by setting $a_{12}=a_{23}=a_{32} = 0$.

7 Conclusions and Future Work

This paper presented a novel self-management model for resource allocation in an autonomic system (AS) comprised of individual, but social, autonomic entities (AEs). Interdependent utilities are utilized to model various social behaviors among the AEs. Each AE can opt to cooperate, hinder or act selfishly towards one or more AEs. Illustrative examples and numerical results show that the presented model is more efficient in a highly dynamic system with varying service demands. Future work will investigate more complex functions for representing the interactions among entities as well as techniques for negotiating the cooperation among the AEs.

References

1. Kephart, J., Chess, D.: The Vision of Autonomic Computing. IEEE Comput. Mag. 36(1), 41–50 (2003)
2. Dobson, S., et al.: A survey of autonomic communications. ACM Trans. Auton. Adapt. Syst. 1(2), 223–259 (2006)
3. Kephart, J., Das, R.: Achieving Self-Management via Utility Functions. IEEE Internet Comput. 11(1), 40–48 (2007)
4. Zhang, J., Yousif, M., Carpenter, R., Figueiredo, R.J.: Application Resource Demand Phase Analysis and Prediction in Support of Dynamic Resource Provisioning. In: 4th intl. conf. Autonomic Computing, 2007. ICAC 2007, pp. 11–15 (June 2007)
5. Kumar, V., Cooper, B., Schwan, K.: Distributed Stream Management using Utility-Driven Self-Adaptive Middleware. In: 2nd intl conf. Autonm. Comput., ICAC 2005, pp. 3–14 (2005)
6. Chess, D.M., Segal, A., Whalley, I., White, S.R.: Unity: experiences with a prototype autonomic computing system. In: intl. conf. Auton, pp. 140–147, May 17–18 (2004)
7. Cohen, J.E.: Cooperation and self-interest: Pareto-inefficiency of Nash equilibria in finite random games. Proc. Natl. Acad. Sci., 95, 9724–9731 (1998)
8. Shall, L.D.: Interdependent Utilities and Pareto Optimality. Quarterly Journal of Economics 86(1), 19–24 (1972)
9. Samaan, N., Karmouch, A.: An Automated Policy Based Management Framework for Differentiated Communication Systems. IEEE J. Sel. Areas Commun. 23(12), 2236–2247 (2005)
10. Xiao, J., Boutaba, R.: QoS-aware service composition and adaptation in autonomic communication. IEEE J. Sel. Areas Commun. 23(12), 2344–2360 (2005)
11. Bandara, A., Lupu, E., Moffet, J., Russo, A.: A Goal-based Approach to Policy Refinement. In: 5th IEEE Wrkshp on Policies for Distributed Systems and Networks (policy 2004)
12. Uttamchandaniand, S., Talcott, C., Pease, D.: Eos: An Approach of Using Behavior Implications for Policy-based Self-management. In: Brunner, M., Keller, A. (eds.) DSOM 2003. LNCS, vol. 2867, pp. 16–27. Springer, Heidelberg (2003)
13. Dowling, J., Curran, E., Cunningham, R., Cahill, V.: Using feedback in collaborative reinforcement learning to adapt and optimise decentralized distributed systems. IEEE Trans. Syst. Man Cybern (Part A) 35(3), 360–372 (2005)
14. Henderson, J., Lemon, O., Georgila, K.: Hybrid Reinforcement/Supervised Learning for Dialogue Policies from COMMUNICATOR data. In: IJCAI workshop on Knowledge and Reasoning in Practical Dialogue Systems (2005)
15. Chiang, F., Braun, R., Hughes, J.: A Biologically Inspired Multi-Agent Framework for Autonomic Service Management. J. Pervasive Comput. Commun. 2(3), 261–275 (2006)
16. Sim, K.M., Sun, W.H.: Ant colony optimization for routing and load-balancing: survey and new directions. IEEE Trans. Syst. Man Cybern (Part A) 33(5), 560–572 (2003)
17. Marshall, I.W., Roadknight, C.M.: Provision of quality of service for active services. Computer Networks 36(1), 75–85 (2001)

Towards an Information Model That Supports Service-Aware, Self-managing Virtual Resources

Claire Fahy[1], Steven Davy[1], Zohra Boudjemil[1], Sven van der Meer[1],
Javier Rubio Loyola[2], Joan Serrat[2], John Strassner[3], Andreas Berl[4],
Hermann de Meer[4], and Daniel Macedo[5]

[1] Telecommunications Software & Systems Group, Waterford, Ireland
[2] Universitat Politècnica de Catalunya, Barcelona, Spain
[3] Motorola Labs, Chicago, IL, USA
[4] University of Passau, Passau, Germany
[5] Laboratoire D'Informatique de Paris 6, Paris, France
cfahy@tssg.org

Abstract. The AUTOI project is creating a virtual communication resource overlay with autonomic characteristics to adapt the services and resources offered to meet changing user needs, business goals, and environmental conditions. Self-knowledge enables the network to reconfigure itself in the face of change to adapt its services according to business goals. The requirements of an information model, to support self-knowledge (concepts, characteristics and behaviour) are presented. This information model plus ontologies provide a common language to represent the self-management of the overlay. This position paper details the requirements in specifying such an information model and language, and describes how the model and language will be used within the project.

Keywords: Information model, service-aware, virtual resource, autonomic management.

1 Motivation and State of the Art

Current voice and data communications networks are difficult to manage, as exemplified by the stovepipe systems that are common in Operational and Business Support Systems. The desire to incorporate best of breed functionality, prohibits the sharing and reuse of common data [1], resulting in an inability to manage the increase in operational, system, and business complexity. Currently, the network is not aware of the needs of the business, so changing business requirements cannot change the services and resources offered by the network.

The AUTOI project [2] uses management overlays that control the virtualisation of network resources and services to implement this mapping of business to network functionality thus resulting in a more optimal use of network resources. Virtual resource overlays can span heterogeneous networks and self-organises according to service requirements. In turn, the deployed services self-configure in response to changes in the overlay. Orchestration mechanisms mediate between different network

S. van der Meer, M. Burgess, and S. Denazis (Eds.): MACE 2008, LNCS 5276, pp. 102–107, 2008.

operations (eg. mobility) enabling conflict resolution and fulfilment of customer requests. Fig.1 depicts the architecture of the AUTOI autonomic control loop. Knowledge is provided by the resources, services, environment, business requirements and relevant context. Orchestration takes this knowledge and reasons over it in order to formulate decisions. Policy based management then enables the self-management of the resources and thus, is governed by the decisions of Orchestration.

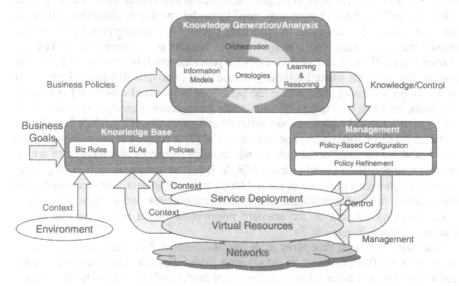

Fig. 1. Components of the AUTOI Autonomic solution

In [2], the AUTOI problem area and strategy were introduced. The next step is to establish requirements for the activities which will realise a solution. To dynamically orchestrate services, a common language is needed that systems can use to express their needs in a machine-programmable manner and translate those needs into a form that the network can understand. This language is built from a single information model, used to define facts and from ontologies, used to augment the facts with additional semantics. The AUTOI model, an extension of the DEN-ng information model [3], captures all necessary concepts concerned with service-oriented virtual resource orchestration. Just as an information model can be refined to guide the development of multiple data models, a common language can be refined to define a set of Domain Specific Languages (DSLs). DSLs are used to address the specific system tasks in an interoperable manner. The combination of the common language and a set of DSLs becomes the source of understanding across the disparate entities of the AUTOI architecture.

Three major information models are widely used today to capture semantics and behaviour of communication networks. The oldest is the Common Information Model (CIM), standardised by the Distributed Management Task Force (DMTF) [4]. Its main focus lies on IT infrastructure including IP networks. CIM provides virtualisation extensions for systems [5] which include a high-level model for various types of platform virtualisation, including hypervisor-based virtualisation, logical and physical partitioning, and operating system containers. However, the CIM specifications for services, networks and resources do not consider resource allocation or associate business goals; thus an autonomic system will find it difficult to respond to context changes. The Shared Information and Data Model (SID) is standardised by the Tele-Management Forum (TM Forum) in [6]. It enables the design of services and network resources in conjunction with products and customers, thus providing the necessary associations to link resources to business activities. It can also be used as a toolkit that allows modellers to select what they need to model specific applications. However, the SID is limited with regard to modelling autonomic environments eg. the policy framework is inflexible and concepts such as context are missing [7]. AUTOI has chosen the DEN-ng model [3] [7]. DEN-ng provides multiple viewpoints of a communications network where business goals are used to govern all managed entities. It defines a policy model that governs the behaviour of managed entities using patterns and roles, enabling it to extensibly administer management functions and data [8]. A policy continuum [3] represents how different constituencies of a product formulate at different levels of abstraction. The context model [7] is coupled to the policy model in order to allow the creation of policies which adapt resources and services to sensed context changes. It was used to build FOCALE [9], an autonomic networking architecture that defines a novel set of control loops that analyse data, compares the current and desired state of a managed entity, and reconfigures accordingly. DEN-ng is currently being adopted as the standard information model within the Autonomic Communications Forum (ACF).

The organisation of this paper is as follows. Section 2 presents the key requirements that AUTOI places on its information model. Section 3 presents some of the early work to extend the DEN-ng information model and the use of the information model within AUTOI. Finally, Section 4 provides a summary and future work.

3 AUTOI Modelling Requirements

In order to derive appropriate modelling requirements, it was necessary to divide the problem into five specific domains for analysis: (1) service, (2) resource and resource virtualisation, (3) management, (4) context, and (5) orchestration.

The information model should provide sufficient abstractions to enable **services** to express their requirements to the management overlay, which then translates those requirements into a particular virtualisation of some or all of the network resources. There are two types of service under analysis: Network and Application. *Network Service (Resource Facing Services in DEN-ng)*, refers to services which network resources provide, such as mobility, QoS, and security. These services depend on the availability and configuration of network resources. Virtualisation enables resources to be collectively treated as a set of programmable building blocks that are used to construct services as directed by the management overlay. *Application Service (Customer Facing Services in DEN-ng)*, refers to the service being offered to the end-user or customer, such as voice and video.

Resources not only refer to physical and logical resources but also virtual resources. The physical and logical resources that provide network services, such as routers or servers, are modelled as virtual resources. Several virtual routers can be created that are associated with a physical router, and the physical topology of the network is then replaced by a virtual topology consisting of one or more overlay networks. These virtual resources are dynamic resources that can be modified to support one or more services running on top of them. This enables a robust and resilient provisioning of virtual resources in case of, e.g., highly loaded routers. The following requirements have been identified for the information model: (1) to serve as a blueprint for defining virtual resources based on higher-level business requirements; (2) enable virtual resources to represent the management of their relationships with their associated physical and logical resources and also their associated network and application services; (3) support mechanisms to define system virtualisation based on classical hypervisors (e.g. XEN); (4) support virtualisation behaviour such as aggregation and splitting of virtual resources; (5) support mechanisms to represent the configuration of virtual network resources, especially virtual routers and the virtual topology.

Management is focussed on provisioning a management plane responsible for enabling the self-management of virtual network and service resources. The model needs to provide concepts that support the following management plane functions: (1) Resource management – usage, availability, (de)composition, virtualisation and assurance – for the self-* functions; (2) Adaptation to changes in network resource mobility, services and resources and direct changes to be made in the appropriate network device configuration and topology; (3) Sharing and reuse of information for self-management functions; (4) Sharing and reuse of information with the virtualisation and orchestration planes; (5) A policy-based framework that is capable of identifying and resolving conflicting goals between different management self-functions as well as between different planes; (6) A policy model that is capable of orchestrating self-organising behaviour using the policy continuum to provide translations between business, network, and implementation policies. The model should support the respective policy transformations.

Given the autonomic interplay between resource and service, handling **contextual** changes in resources and services is vital. In addition, user requirements and environmental conditions can change without warning. This implies that such potential changes must be continually inspected with respect to business objectives. Contextual abstractions in the following areas need to be provided as part of the information model: (1) Resource (Network & Service), (2) Service (Network & Application), (3) Network (Virtual, Physical & Logical) and (4) Business Requirements.

The **Orchestration** function co-ordinates and mediates between multiple types of network services and functions such as mobility, security and QoS. Intelligent components are *orchestrated* according to the current context (resource or service), changes in high level objectives (user needs and business goals), and environmental conditions [10]. Orchestration is dependent on the relationships between the concepts discussed previously including: (1)Management & Context – A change in context will cause the orchestration function to analyse management tasks – their dependencies and ordering - in order to reconfigure the self-* components; (2) Service & Resource – changes in either entity may require re-configuration or re-organisation of that entity and/or the other entity.

4   Defining and Using the AUTOI Information Model

We take the current DEN-ng information model as the basis for the information model. The problem domain only requires a subset of DEN-ng thus only particulars associated with the domains service, resource, management and context will be retained. This subset is then extended with concepts that are specific to the virtualisation requirements. These extensions will be submitted to the ACF for future standardisation.

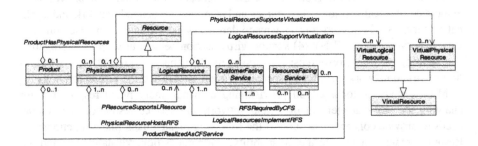

Fig. 2. Product-Service-Resource and Virtual Resource Relationships

Fig 2 illustrates an example of one subset of the early model. It demonstrates the representation of the mapping of the business goals towards resource allocation. This is achieved through the linkage of product (*the product procured by the customer*) to service (*customer facing* to *resource facing*) onto resource (virtual, logical and physical). The product-service-resource relationships come directly from DEN-ng, while the new concepts of *VirtualResource* and its relevant relationships have been added. The information model will be used primarily as a source of concepts for a set of DSLs [11]. A DSL is an abstraction mechanism which handles the complexity in a given domain by providing a customised programming language that represents concepts and rules specific to that application domain enabling developers to work directly with domain concepts. The AUTOI common language will be used to generate 3 domain-specific DSLs - service, resource and management.

5   Summary and Future Work

An information model that will support the self-management of a service-oriented virtual resource overlay is under creation in AUTOI. A subset of the DEN-ng information model is used as the basis for representing business goals, services, logical and physical resources, policy management and context awareness. DEN-ng is being extended, to create the AUTOI information model, to include appropriate resource and service virtualisation concepts, along with management models to orchestrate the virtualisation process. The resulting model and associated ontologies will be used to generate DSLs in the areas of service, resource and management. Future work in the AUTOI project will include the validation of the generated DSLs (and thus the extensions to the information model) against defined scenarios in the areas of seamless mobility management and service assurance.

Acknowledgements

This research activity is funded under the EU IST FP7 project, *Autonomic Internet* (Grant agreement no.:216404).

References

1. Strassner, J., Menich, B.J.: Philosophy and methodology for knowledge discovery in auto-nomic computing systems. In: Proceedings. Sixteenth International Workshop on Database and Expert Systems Applications, August 22-26, pp. 738–743 (2005)
2. Bassi, A., Denazis, S., Galis, A., Fahy, C., Serrano, M., Serrat, J.: Autonomic Internet: A Perspective for Future Internet Services Based on Autonomic Principles. In: Proc. of 2nd IEEE International Workshop on Modelling Autonomic Communications (MACE), San José, California, USA (2007)
3. Strassner, J.: Policy Based Network Management. Morgan Kaufman, San Francisco; ISBN 1-55860-859-1
4. DMTF, CIM Schema: Version 2.18,
   http://www.dmtf.org/standards/cim/cim_schema_v218/
5. DMTF, CIM System Virtualization Model White Paper, DSP 2013, Version 1.0.0 (No-vember 2007)
6. TMF (Shared Information/Data (SID) Model - Business View Concepts, Principles, and Domains. GB922, Ed. NGOSS R6.1, Document Version 6.1 (November 2005)
7. Strassner, J., Samudrala, S., Cox, G., Liu, Y., Jiang, M., Zhang, J., van der Meer, S., Foghlú, M.Ó., Donnelly, W.: The Design of a New Context-Aware Policy Model for Autonomic Networking. In: 5th IEEE International Conference on Autonomic Computing (ICAC), June 2-6, Chicago, Illinois (2008)
8. Davy, S., Jennings, B., Strassner, J.: Conflict Prevention via Model-driven Policy Refine-ment. In: State, R., van der Meer, S., O'Sullivan, D., Pfeifer, T. (eds.) DSOM 2006. LNCS, vol. 4269, pp. 209–220. Springer, Heidelberg (2006)
9. Strassner, J., Agoulmine, N., Lehtihet, E.: FOCALE - A Novel Autonomic Networking Architecture. In: Proc. of Latin American Autonomic Computing Symposium (LAACS), Campo Grande, MS, Brazil (2006)
10. Strassner, J., Foghlú, Ó., Donnelly, M., Agoulmine, W.,, N.: Beyond the Knowledge Plane: An Inference Plane to support the Next Generation Internet. In: Proc. of First Inter-national Global Information Infrastructure Symposium (GIIS), Marrakech, Morocco, July 2-6, pp. 112–119 (2007)
11. Kelly, S., Tolvanen, J.: Domain Specific Modelling – Enabling Full Code Generation. Wiley, Chichester (2008)

A Domain-Specific Modelling Approach
for Autonomic Network Management

Brian Pickering[1], Miguel A. Fernández[2], Antonio Castillo[2],
and Erhan Mengusoglu[1]

[1] Pervasive & Advanced Messaging Technologies
IBM Hursley, UK
{brian_pickering,mengusog}@uk.ibm.com
[2] Tools & Services for Online Access & Customer Networks
Telefónica Research & Development – Valladolid, Spain
{mafg,acp07}@tid.es

Abstract. This paper describes IBM's and Telefónica's joint work in progress in the field of Domain-Specific Modelling applied to Autonomic Network Management in the context of the European IST FP6 project MODELPLEX. In modelling edge-of-network devices which act as service access points from consumers to the telephone network, we have introduced a dynamic aspect to the network topology which affects the way Service Level Agreements (SLAs) should be modelled and processed within an autonomic management control loop. It is suggested that it is not possible to separate system and rule for managing services across a service-provider network.

Keywords: Autonomic computing; system management; domain-specific modelling.

1 Introduction

When it comes to understanding, creating and managing complex systems, a convenient and succinct way of representing systems is necessary. A good abstraction should capture all and only that information which is vital for the understanding of the underlying system, either in terms of structure or behaviour or both. Abstractions of this kind may be seen as models which provide "a description or specification of that system and its environment for some certain purpose" [11]. The work reported here represents initial attempts to model the required components and activities associated with the automated management of network services.

Much has been written about the increasingly complex challenges facing service providers, in terms of management objects (service or network [12]) and the constraining rules and policies (associated with charging [13], for instance), as well as related to the ever-changing consumer environment [6].

Appropriate modelling can help service providers in this respect ([10], [2]), with Service Oriented Architectures ([9], [10], [12]) and policy management ([9]) as key focus areas. This renders modelling service management ([3]) and providing the necessary tooling and domain-specific approaches ([2]) particularly pertinent. But there

S. van der Meer, M. Burgess, and S. Denazis (Eds.): MACE 2008, LNCS 5276, pp. 108–113, 2008.
© Springer-Verlag Berlin Heidelberg 2008

has been little consideration of how to integrate a model-driven approach – in terms of developing structural and behavioural abstractions for the design and operation of service delivery platforms (see [9], for example) – either with increasingly popular autonomic concepts ([1], [6]) or with appropriate representations of the network and service elements to be managed. If possible, unifying the managed infrastructure with the delivered services would, it seems, provide some benefit for management and service development.

Whilst testing and approving an autonomic approach, González et al have described the challenges presented to service providers in respect of modelling edge-of-network devices [6]. Wong et al concentrate instead on the complexity of the multi-layered management task as represented by the FCAPS proposals, preferring in the end the eTOM framework [12]. They devote little attention though to managing policies and constraints. The latter is a significant issue, which Wong and co-workers hint at with reference to Web Services. Given this, there is a need for efficient representation which, according to Xu and Jennings [13] as well as Barrett et al [2], is best handled via domain-specific language definition.

Against this background, we have begun to evaluate the benefits of an internally derived DSL for edge-of-network device modelling as described in the next section. In parallel, we have begun to investigate the benefits of management automation using autonomic concepts as set out below and with a specific focus on service management via Service Level Agreement (SLA) processing. We must, however, consider what if any the implications are of applying this management approach to our edge-of-network device models within service delivery.

2 Domain Specific Languages for Network Description

Especially in the case of network management, where the system under consideration is a complex network delivering services to private subscribers via a range of different devices, we need an adequate language to capture and represent network components. The Common Information Model (CIM) [4] provides a useful starting point, notwithstanding the more recent Common Model Library proposals which are more specifically geared towards IT services [3]. Although not directly compliant with the Unified Modeling Language (UML) meta-model, the CIM meta-model's concepts can be mapped to the Meta Object Facility (MOF) or other meta-models, like Ecore, so that CIM-like models can be created in UML or in the Eclipse Modelling Framework (EMF), as in our case. An example of this kind of mapping is shown in [5] where a UML profile for CIM is presented jointly by the DMTF and the OMG.

Starting from a transformation of CIM into the Ecore meta-model the aim is to build a graphical DSL by creating higher-level abstractions using model composition techniques, with the help of the Reuseware Composition Framework [7] and also enriching the meta-model with domain rules expressed in the Object Constraint Language (OCL) [8]. This approach offers great flexibility, as it is not dependent on any particular higher-level meta-model. This flexibility will also be useful at runtime, when the network models need to be updated to cater for changes in the network configuration and composition, as discussed in the next section.

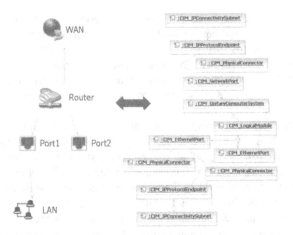

Fig. 1. An example of a router modelled with a DSL and the same model expressed in UML

An important motivation for investigating graphical DSLs at all is to allow us to prove how a simplified representation might support different OSS and BSS functions. Commercial experts, for instance, may not be considered well versed in network element management, and yet still need to understand the implications of element change for the development of their services. Figure 1 shows initial attempts to represent the edge-of-network devices. To the right of the figure, as stated above, we have mapped the DSL representation to a UML-like presentation of CIM.

The immediate benefits of this representation include: (a) the automatic generation of the device configuration specifications required to support new and proposed services by means of Model-to-model transformation techniques and tools, such as the ATLAS Transformation Language (ATL) [14]; (b) current services can be more readily deployed to new devices; (c) we enable the development of a common framework of existing components which may extend into operational and other lifecycle management considerations; and (d) the ability to interact with the other parts of the management system, and especially the operational knowledge-base, as described in the next section. We need to consider the specific implications of including the device model into the management process.

3 Models for Automated Network Management

The Autonomic Computing Initiative (ACI) promoted by IBM (see [1]) has proposed a control loop of management processes – MAPE (monitoring, analysing, planning and execution) – based on knowledge (K), both historical and as specified in management rules and policies.

Figure 2 shows the model of the MAPE management processes within the context of a generalised system-management meta-model also developed within the MODELPLEX project. The model shows a conceptual separation amongst management elements of system management process steps (*MAPE Phase*), the elements to be managed (*ManagedEntity*, in this case the service delivered to the consumer across the network) and management knowledge.

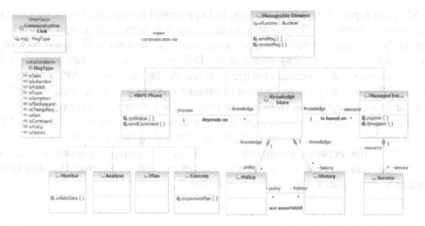

Fig. 2. Proposed model of the MAPE-K control loop

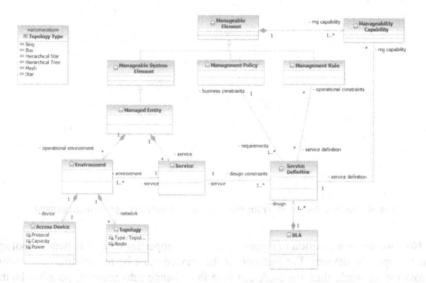

Fig. 3. A possible model for service level agreements (SLAs)

Apart from the historical data – that is the accumulation and aggregation of information about the current system – within the *Knowledge Store*, the *Policy* class is key: this is what determines how the service is maintained and monitored. Figure 3 extends the *Policy* concept as it relates to management rules. Here we see that the constraints against which services are managed (the service level agreements) contain at least a set of definitions relating to the desired function of the service or services. The current formalism being considered relates directly to work with web services (see for instance [12]). The SLA, or contract between service provider and consumer, contains the service definitions, but has only indirect access to information about the service environment.

With this separation, service function and operational environment are segregated for management purposes. This seems counter-intuitive to some degree with network operation. We highlighted above that all operational and business staff should be able to use the network model encapsulated in the DSL we are currently developing for the express purposes of automatic configuration and deployment (the MAPE processes of Plan and Execute) and the deployment of existing services to new devices, so it is clear that our SLA concept has to include some reference to the operational environment.

Aligning the DSL work and modelling the management process suggests that the initial MAPE-K model must be modified in terms of service management to include an explicit link between environment and SLA. Processing the customer contract must, then, take account of topological changes as well as the characteristics of the various access devices. This is shown in Figure 4.

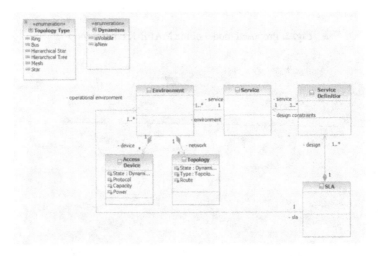

Fig. 4. Model enhancements for runtime edge-of-network device management

Now we are in a position to represent dynamic properties both of network topology and the specific devices. For instance, if the service must be rerouted for any reason across the network, then the SLA can take this change into account, possibly laying greater emphasis on certain monitoring data or constraints. Similarly, if a consumer changes or updates a device, then any knock-on effects for the SLA can be picked up and processed.

The state information is now directly accessible to the SLA. So although a service definition may remain relatively static, in that it will only change if planned service modification is to take place, the service can still be managed at runtime in terms of quality and so forth whilst taking into account any and all changes to the operational environment.

Service definition and the dynamism of the operational environment were not represented in the initial MAPE-based service management model in Figure 3. With the modifications shown in Figure 4, we can now move forward in allowing full control and flexibility to the autonomic management of services.

4 Next Steps

Having outlined the service management approach and begun to model features of the network in terms which can be understood by all operational and commercial staff, we now need to investigate further the implications and benefits of an explicit link between SLA processing and operational environment.

Acknowledgments. The work presented in this paper is being carried out in the context of the MODELPLEX project (IST-FP6-2006 Contract No. 34081).

References

1. Autonomic Computing, http://www-03.ibm.com/autonomic/
2. Barrett, K., Davy, S., Strassner, J., Jennings, B., van der Meer, S., Donnelly, W.: A Model Based Approach for Policy Tool Generation and Policy Analysis. In: Proc. 1st IEEE Global Information Infrastructure Symposium (GIIS 2007), pp. 99–105. IEEE, Los Alamitos (2007)
3. Common Model Library specification, http://www.ibm.com/software/sw-library/en_US/detail/G587418G25075S71.html/
4. DMTF's Common Information Model Website, http://www.dmtf.org/standards/cim/
5. DMTF, UML Profile for CIM, Preliminary Standard, http://www.dtmf.org/standards/published_documents/DSP0219.pdf
6. González, J., et al.: Self-adapted Service Offering for Residential Environments. In: 1st IEEE Workshop on Autonomic Communications and Network Management (ACNM 2007) (2007)
7. Reuseware Composition Framework Website, http://www.reuseware.org/
8. Object Constraint Language (OCL) Specification from the OMG, Version 2.0, http://www.omg.org/cgi-bin/doc?formal/2006-05-01
9. Maes, S.: Service Delivery Platforms as IT Realization of OMA Service Environment: Service Oriented Architectures for Telecommunications. In: WCNC 2007. IEEE, Los Alamitos (2007)
10. Mengusoglu, E. and Pickering, J.: Specific meta-models for real-time distributed device management (unpublished), http://www.modelplex.org/
11. Object Management Group. MDA Guide Version 1.0.1 (2003), http://www.omg.org/cgi-bin/apps/doc?omg/03-06-01.pdf
12. Wong, D., Ting, C., Yeh, C.: From Network Management to Service Management – A Challenge to Telecom Service Providers. In: Proc. 2nd International Conference on Innovative Computing, Information and Control (ICICIC 2007) (2007)
13. Xu, L., Jennings, B.: Automating the Generation, Deployment and Application Charging Schemes for Composed IMS Services. In: Proc. 10th IFIP/IEEE International Symposium on Integrated Network Management (IM 2007) 10(1), 856–859 (2007)
14. Jouault, F., Kurtev, I.: Transforming Models with the ATL. In: Bruel, J.-M. (ed.) MoDELS 2005. LNCS, vol. 3844, pp. 128–138. Springer, Heidelberg (2006)

Autonomic Provisioning Model for Digital Home Services

José A. Lozano[1], Alfonso Castro[1], Juan M. González[1], Jorge E. López de Vergara[2], Víctor A. Villagrá[3], and Vicente Olmedo[3]

[1] Telefónica Investigación y Desarrollo, Emilio Vargas 6, 28043-Madrid, Spain
{jal,acast,jmgm}@tid.es
[2] Universidad Autónoma de Madrid, Francisco Tomás y Valiente 11, 28049, Madrid, Spain
jorge.lopez_vergara@uam.es
[3] Universidad Politécnica de Madrid, Avda. Complutense s/n, 28040, Madrid, Spain
{villagra,volmedo}@dit.upm.es

Abstract. Digital Home services provisioning is becoming one of the main challenges for telecommunications operators as the heterogeneity and complexity of end users devices grows dramatically. Moreover, home network topology and composition can be changed by end users without any control from the service provider side.

Traditional centralized management paradigms are not valid for this kind of dynamic and unpredictable environments as they have been thought for more static scenarios. Autonomic Communication (AC) can help in solving this problems building a knowledge based management solution for this scenario. Autonomic Agents are able to locally deal with most of the configuration tasks as they use inference to decide the most suitable device configuration. This paper shows an autonomic provisioning model for the dynamic configuration of end user devices. The model is validated by a proof of concept.

Keywords: Autonomic Communication, self-provisioning, knowledge-based management.

1 Introduction

Telecommunications and Information Technologies are having a deep impact in the home environment. Nowadays, users are demanding new and more attractive services focused on comfort, entertainment, security, e-health, etc. A first consequence is that of the growing variety of networked intelligent devices appearing at homes. These devices range from simple sensors to more complex ones as computers, video consoles, set top boxes, routers, etc. that require to be configured for the services deployed on them. This scenario is far from the traditional telecommunications services environment in which the end devices configuration is independent of the services and therefore any configuration is necessary at service provisioning time. For this reason, Digital Home service provisioning is becoming one of the main challenges for telecommunications companies because it is a labour intensive process with a direct impact in the Operating Expenses (OPEX). But, even for end users, these services

S. van der Meer, M. Burgess, and S. Denazis (Eds.): MACE 2008, LNCS 5276, pp. 114–119, 2008.

could require some skills in Information Technologies that could become a barrier for the deployment of new services.

One of the keys to take a good position in residential environment is to offer services easy to configure, use and manage. The concept of "one click provisioning" means that the only need for customers is to know about services without thinking on devices and their configuration. Moreover, the service provision process should be transparent to the user. But another challenge arises since the composition and topology of physical and logical resources are defined and modified directly by users. As a consequence of this situation, there will be a different environment for each customer requiring an individual management solution.

This paper is based on the work presented in [2]. The principal goal of the former research was to personalize the service offer for a specific user whereas the work presented in this paper is more focused on self configuration and self diagnosis of devices when it is associated with a service. The definition of a new provisioning model arises from such approach.

The remainder of this paper is organised as follows. Section 2 states how autonomic principles have been used to generate a new provisioning model for Digital Home services. Section 3 shows how knowledge technologies, mainly ontologies and policies, have been applied in the project. In section 4 a proof of concept that validates the exposed principles and ideas is described. Finally, a section including some conclusions is presented in order to plan further work in this area.

2 The Autonomic Approach for Digital Home Services Configuration

The model that is proposed in this paper uses Autonomic Communications concepts and principles to built Autonomous Agents (AA) that are responsible for the management tasks of a Digital Home and they will act according to the domain knowledge and goals described by the operator.

The autonomous agents developed for the proof of concept follow the typical monitoring, analysis, planning and execute closed loop architecture. This architecture was presented by IBM in [4] and has been further enhanced by FOCALE [5].

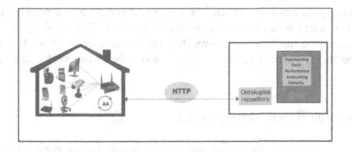

Fig. 1. AA communication with ISP

FOCALE uses policies to conduit the autonomic closed loop behavior and adds a module for learning.

Two functional elements stand out in the proposed architecture for the autonomous agent depicted in Figure 2:

- The **semantic-based service management** component (Autonomous Agent). For this component to fulfil its tasks it is necessary to define its knowledge domain. That is information about the service catalogue together with the capabilities that are required, devices' descriptions with their associated capabilities, users' preferences, operator's policies and so on. With all this information, the agent will recommend services to the user according to the devices connected to the network at any given time and will also provide their correct configuration. As a result device configuration complexity is hidden,
- The **devices management** component (Middleware). It is the interface with devices. This block is responsible for device monitoring and configuration. Moreover, this component acts as a middleware element that translates the device semantic description to a language that the devices can understand and vice versa.

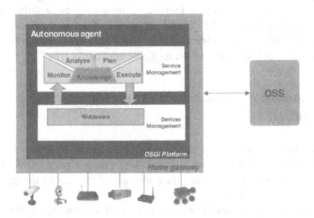

Fig. 2. Autonomous element architecture

It is important to highlight the relevance of the knowledge layer. This layer is implemented using an ontology, which is a semantic description in a machine readable format that is shared by all the entities of the architecture. This ontology in combination with inference mechanisms allows the configuration of devices. A further description on the knowledge plane, ontologies and policies can be found in the next section.

3 Knowledge Based Management

Knowledge is the core of the model and the responsible for the correct work of the whole architecture. Knowledge enables agents to interpret their context and it also provides information exchange support between entities. For a machine to automatically understand and interpret the information, it is necessary to add a semantic description to traditional Information Models. For this purpose, an ontology has been used in the proof of concept.

Through the concepts defined in the ontology, it is possible for the agent to understand what a service is, how it is related to devices, which is the best configuration for a specific service, user preferences and so on. Furthermore, through rules definition it is possible to fit more than technical aspects, because commercial and strategic requirements together with user preferences can also be introduced into the rules resulting in highly personalised services.

3.1 Ontologies

As it has been stated before, an ontology has been used to create a semantic model including service, device and configuration issues. This ontology establishes a knowledge plane to allow customers and service providers to share the same environment's description.

The model is depicted in Figure 3 shows the main concepts that have been described in the semantic model developed for the proof of concept. It can be observed that each service is linked with the devices' capabilities required to deploy the service. Devices are also linked with their best configuration to fulfil a particular service. Devices are referred in the model as abstract entities, this concept does not represent a specific model of camera, but the service involved characteristics.

In the proof of concept, the ontology has been defined in OWL [6] using Protegé [8] as editor to implement the ontology and SWRL [7] to define the inference rules. Bossam [10] has been used as the inference engine,

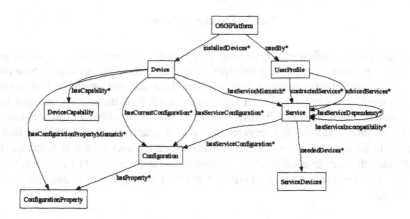

Fig. 3. Ontology defined for the autonomous agent

3.2 Reasoning Rules

The behavioural model is built through the use of policies. These policies will tell how the infrastructure must behave. The specification of how services relate with a specific customers commercial segment may be an example of this situation. Any service may be technically suitable for a specific user, but it may make no commercial sense to offer him such a service. This commercial behaviour is accomplished through policy description.

In the proof of concept policies are materialized within the semantic model as a set of SWRL rules.

4 Proof of Concept Description

The proof of concept consists of a digital home with two devices: a camera and a router and a service catalogue composed of three services: Colour Tele-surveillance, Black&White Tele-surveillance, Night Tele-surveillance. It will be shown that users can enjoy services without being involved in technical configuration issues. Figure 4 shows the schema of the proof of concept.

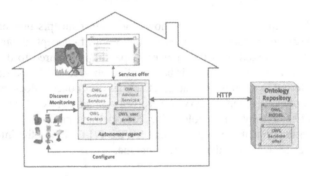

Fig. 4. Provisioning process

The use case workflow can be summarized as follows: every time the agent detects changes in the context settings, it analyzes them according to the policies. These policies are generated by the operator from high-level services configuration policies and they are used by the system to infer knowledge. Each time the context changes by a user action or a new service being offered by the Service Provider, a local web page is updated to show the users the services they can contract. This web could be further enriched to become a Customer Service Web. When the user contracts a service, the agent plans the correct configuration of devices for this service. The case where parameters are corrected when any fault in a device's configuration is detected is also considered.

5 Conclusions and Further Work

The Information Services and the devices in future home environments are more complex than current ones. The management of such environments supposes a challenge for Telecommunications companies as they are very dynamic and unpredictable and current management architectures are designed to cope with more static and controlled scenarios.

One of the main advantages of this model is that it works on a common, shared service level. This prevents end users from having any technical skills. On the other hand, operator technicians will be freed from some configuration tasks by working once harder in the definition services phases.

Regarding configuration tasks, devices are modeled as a set of capabilities and services are related to the capabilities that are required. This fact will enable the agent to make relations between specific devices and the configuration that has to be applied for a specific service.

Furthermore, next steps will imply further work on diagnosis and fault resolutions, since these management disciplines will help users to overcome problem when they occur. Security and privacy are other important issues to be considered as the autonomic agents have to be deployed on devices located in residential environments.

References

1. Smirnov, M.: Autonomic Communication, Research Agenda for a New Communication Paradigm Autonomic Communication. White Paper (November 2004)
2. Gonzalez, J.M., Lozano, J.A., López, J., Villagrá, V.: Self-adapted Service Offering for Residential Environment. In: IEEE IM-ACNM 2007 Proceedings, München (May 2007)
3. OSGi Alliance: About the OSGi Service Platform. Technical White Paper Revision 4.1 (November 11, 2005)
4. Kephart, J.O., Chess, D.M.: The Vision of Autonomic Computing. IEEE Computer Society, IBM Thomas J. Watson Research Center (January 2003)
5. Strassner, J.C., Agoulmine, N., Lehtihet, E.: FOCALE – A Novel Autonomic Networking Architecture. In: Proceedings of Latin American Autonomic Computing Symposium (LAACS), Campo Grande, MS, Brazil, July 18-19 (2006)
6. McGuinness, D.L., van Harmelen, F.: OWL Web Ontology Language Overview. W3C Recommendation (February 10, 2004)
7. Horrocks, I., Patel-Schneider, P.F., Boley, H., Tabel, S., Grosof, B., Dean, M.: SWRL: A Semantic Web Rule Language Combining OWL and RuleML. W3C Member Submission (May 21, 2004)
8. Knublauch, H., Fergerson, R.W., Noy, N.F., Musen, M.A.: The Protégé OWL Plugin: An Open Development Environment for Semantic Web Applications. In: Third International Semantic Web Conference, Hiroshima, Japan (2004)
9. Apache Tomcat, http://www.tomcat.apache.org/
10. Jang, M., Sohn, J.-C.: Bossam: An extended Rule Engine for OWL Inferencing. In: Antoniou, G., Boley, H. (eds.) RuleML 2004. LNCS, vol. 3323, pp. 128–138. Springer, Heidelberg (2004)

SLA e-Negotiations, Enforcement and Management in an Autonomic Environment

Giannis Koumoutsos[1], Spyros Denazis[1,2], and Kleanthis Thramboulidis[1]

[1] University of Patras
[2] Hitachi Europe
{koumouts,sdena,thrambo}@ece.upatras.gr

Abstract. The process of SLA acquisition, enforcement and management nowadays includes mostly manual, time-consuming processes both on end-users' and ISPs' side. We need to automate processes and enable real e-Negotiations between end-users and ISPs as well as between ISPs. Ontology based information and knowledge modeling involved in SLA e-Negotiation, Enforcement and Management is presented in this paper. Multiple layers of understanding of a complete SLA are presented on the end-users' application based selection, as well as in the ISPs' side through multiple layers of the policy continuum. Dynamic mappings and translation through model based ontology alignment in Knowledge Bases will use this knowledge to automatically configure network elements.

1 Introduction

The rapid growth of the internet resulted in the proliferation of services and technologies comprising a complex network mosaic of various access methods, protocols, frequency bands, data speeds, and core transport networks. Communication services are inflexible in nature, manually deployed and managed, requiring highly labor-intensive support structures, with consequent inflexibility and time consuming human involved processes.

In order for the ISPs to enforce the negotiated Service Level Agreements (SLAs) which include provided services' QoS characteristics, they will need to configure network devices and manage QoS in a multi-vendor environment. Autonomic Networking seeks to reduce human intervention in the management process especially in the lower levels through the use of control loops that continuously re-configure the system to keep its behavior within desired bounds.

Knowledge within models is used by policy-based network management systems [1], incorporating dynamic translations to automatically configure network elements in response to changing user requirements, environmental context and business goals. Policy continuum provides a framework for the development of models and policy languages, tied together by a common information model, each targeting a different layer of abstraction. In [2] a formal model is presented for the five views of the policy continuum: Business, System, Administrator, Device and Instance. Further analysis of the policy continuum is presented in [1] as part of DEN-ng information model, an

S. van der Meer, M. Burgess, and S. Denazis (Eds.): MACE 2008, LNCS 5276, pp. 120–125, 2008.

approach that is also adopted in this paper. A prototype implementation of FOCALE architecture based on DEN-ng model is presented in [3].

In self-managing systems, ontologies can play an important role, as they enable components to reason about themselves in their specific environment. This is a necessary first step in enabling systems to become self-aware and self-configuring, and from there self-healing and self-optimizing. Prior research work has studied their applicability to represent the management information definitions [4], the mapping processes [5] for semantic integration and the representation of behavior and policy definitions [6].

Policies representing system state, requirements and intent are used in [7] to negotiate agreements between mutually unknown and untrusted systems. The minimum requirement is a shared common ontology based on a common conceptualization of the domain. In [8] a good survey is presented of the protocols that have been proposed for facilitating dynamic service negotiations in the next-generation internet: RNAP, SrNP, COPS-SLS, DSNP, QoS-NSLP and QoS-GSLP.

In [9] an expressive framework is proposed of adequate knowledge representation (KR) concepts, upon which a declarative XML-based language is build called Rule Based Service Level Agreement (RBSLA) for interchange, serialization and verification of rules. Finally a complete tool for Service level Management is presented (RBSLM).

In this paper we will use information modeling based on ontologies to capture knowledge relating to user preference, network capabilities, environmental constraints and business policies in an SLA between an end-user and an ISP and between ISPs. Ontological engineering will provide us with the so much needed inference capabilities. Policy-based network management systems incorporating translation through model based ontology alignment will use this knowledge to automatically configure network elements in response to changing requirements and context. We focus on some key points in the concept of autonomous network management that will provide us with an architecture upon which a complete negotiation framework such as the one described in [10] can be deployed.

After presenting the framework architecture in section 2, SLA Modeling and Representation issues are analyzed both from the end-user's and the provider's point of view in section 3. Section 4, concludes this paper and future work is presented.

2 The Framework

SLA e-negotiations involve end-users and ISPs trying to reach an agreement in multiple bilateral interactions (Figure 1). From there ISPs can dynamically negotiate with other ISPs in order to provide their customers with competitive proposals.

A Knowledge Base (KB) was adopted to get the means for the computerized collection, organization, and retrieval of knowledge involved in our domain. Service Oriented Architecture (SOA) was used towards automation and flexibility accommodating all appropriate services involved in our application domain. It provides the dynamically created negotiation Semantic Web Service (SWS) based interfaces and a complete approach on locating and invoking services that implement activities for the negotiation and management processes.

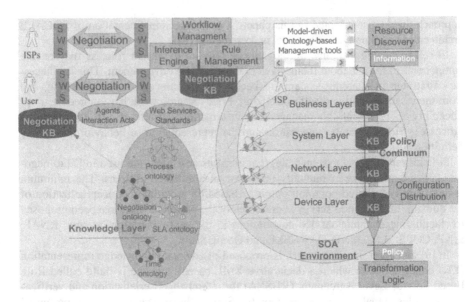

Fig. 1. SLA e-Negotiations, Enforcement and Management framework

The knowledge layer is a common access repository containing pre-specified ontologies modelling the domain. The structure and vision of these common knowledge ontologies will be the guide to solve communication and interoperability issues. Ontology alignment, mapping [11] and merging knowledge will also be included in this repository possibly in the form of widely acceptable Alignment Files for machine and human processing. For accessing these repositories again SWS can be used.

Each layer is depicted with a separate KB containing layer specific models and knowledge. The Resource Discovery module obtains information from the different layers in the policy continuum that affect SLA negotiation and management. Carefully defined Models formalized in ontologies for human and machine processing is the key for getting simple information to the knowledge level each layer needs, in order to reason on the appropriate behavior.

Transformation Logic takes policies from the higher layers and with model mappings through ontology alignment brings their effects until the device layer. Each layer is responsible for striping the request of the appropriate for this layer information and forwarding the request to the lower layer. When a layer receives a request translates it to whatever this request means for this layer using the context and situation aware self-knowledge.

3   SLA Modeling and Representation

Our approach on SLA modeling uses ontologies formalized in Ontology Web Language (OWL) and Semantic Web Rule Language (SWRL) for rule editing. ISPs need to manage a greater number of SLAs than they used to, which needs new levels of flexibility and automation not available with the current approaches. The complexity of SLAs, services, network environments, access technologies and end-user devices requires new forms of knowledge representation to automatically draw inferences in order to manage and enforce contractual agreements.

Our declarative rule-based approach provides several advantages. The formalization of SLA specifications as logic programs is a lot closer to human understanding and way of thinking and designing systems. ECA rules are a very easy way to gradually specify a system even for not computer familiars from the more general to exceptions and vice versa. Still the code remains executable by a generic inference engine producing new knowledge to your expert system or actions for further execution. The traceability of such systems is proven as well as their ability to detect and resolve conflicting knowledge using defeasible logics. Extensibility is the main advantage by simply adding new rules and verifying your system with no need of intervening and correcting procedural programs. Automated rule chaining aids in compact knowledge representation as well as flexibility to adapt to rapidly changing business requirements. Incorporating executable procedural programs within the capabilities of a working inference engine such as JESS used in our prototype implementation is also very important. It provides a way of implementing reusable, with well described semantics activities, to be dynamically used by our system. Clear semantics provided by information modeling and formalization by ontology engineering is an important requirement in logical programming.

3.1 End User SLA Specifics

The end-users will need an end-to-end guaranteed SLA described right to their level of understanding, and transparent to the networking environment that multiple ISPs construct nowadays. The understanding level for a complete SLA description is not common to all users and usually depends on the knowledge they possess, mainly on the QoS characteristics of the SLA they are looking for.

Typically the user search for an SLA based on the application he wants to be in position to deploy and not any other engineering level details. Most users are not familiar with the networking technical details in order to specify the QoS of an SLA in terms of bandwidth, jitter, latency etc. They are also not very confident about the different wired and mobile network technologies that greatly influence the choices in a specific environment. Even for the devices they will use to connect most have limited knowledge of their differences in capabilities and performance in specific applications. The access service is only an obstacle that must be removed for the user to access internet services and information's.

Keeping this point of view we approached SLA modeling for the end user differently than other approaches. Our model for user's preference elicitation and SLA selection is based on the well understood applications each user wants to deploy. For that we will need to create service profiles that will dynamically match application layer service requirements. As applications and network technologies evolve so does the mapping between application and network layer QoS models.

Cost restrictions and the selection of the applications to be deployed are what the user will need to balance. These preferences must also be in accordance with the access network characteristics and end user device hardware and software capabilities.

In order to achieve that, the modeling of the access network and device characteristics and the flexible mapping around the application based user preference was our choice.

By providing the application based layer of abstraction to end-users selection we reach an upper level of Goal-based policy for SLA selection [12]. This permits greater flexibility and frees end-users from having to know low-level system function details, at the cost of requiring sophisticated modeling. Our KB will drive decision inside the restrictions of the specific device and network capabilities.

3.2 Providers SLA Specifics

Negotiations between ISPs are based on a "language" that ISPs will use in their e-negotiations to describe agreements. The concepts of this language are formulated in an ontology and will include the relationship with user level QoS concepts. That is because ISPs need to understand users' language for expressing their preferred SLAs and automatically translate these preferences to their internal SLA model. ISPs will need to walk down the policy continuum translating the SLA to the specifics of each layer in order to negotiate based on their resources and enforce and manage after negotiation.

Based on the policy continuum an SLA describes different things for each layer. In order for each layer to correctly decide the ability to enforce a specific SLA at a specific time and situation it must be context aware and receive an understandable to this layer SLA description. For the layer-compatible SLA description, an SLA specification for each layer and the automated dynamic mapping to the neighboring layers must be provided. For the context and situation aware a complete model that will include the static and dynamic characteristics of the layer is very important.

For the business layer Cost is a combination of the Class of Service (CoS) and other things that must be taken in account like: compensations required in case of failure, specifics on days and time where different CoS is required and so forth. Encoding all these in our KB in the form of rules would require a great number of rules that would lead to complicated specification. The role of Utility functions [12] in automated decision making is to save as from these situations. ISPs unlike end-users can afford policy authors to specify a multidimensional set of preferences that are difficult to elicit.

The System layer will understand the same fuzzy CoS and its role will be to combine it with capabilities and resources of the system to examine the SLAs applicability. For that it will 'ask' the network by sending network layer SLA specifics. In order for the Network layer to understand what it is been asked to verify, the system will translate general SLA requirements to end-to-end QoS paths with their characteristics. The Network will receive this understandable requirement and will translate it to Device layer requirements and send them to local PDPs and from there to devices.

4   Conclusions and Future Work

In this paper an approach that uses ontology-based information modeling to capture knowledge pertaining to user preferences, network capabilities, environmental constraints and business policies is presented. Ontological engineering can provide us with solutions in interoperability, Knowledge formalization, alignment, inference and reasoning issues. The goal of ontology-based network management is to solve the tower of Babel situation and to improve the manageability of network resources through the application of formal ontologies. This will unleash the automated SLA e-Negotiation between end-users and ISPs and between ISPs.

With automated e-negotiations there is a potential risk that the overall process and the business outcomes may become somewhat unpredictable. We need workflow management and visualization for administrators to control multiple processes. We are currently working on an appropriate graphical workflow management approach for both SLA negotiation and management.

Acknowledgements. This work has been co-funded in part from the European Union by 75% and from the Hellenic State by 25% through the Operational Program Competitiveness, 2000-2006, in the context of PENED 2003 03ED723 project.

References

1. Strassner, J.: Policy Based Network Management. Morgan Kaufman, San Francisco; ISBN 1-55860-859-1
2. Van der Meer, S., Davy, S., Carroll, R., Jennings, B., Strassner, J.: Autonomic Networking: Prototype Implementation of the Policy Continuum In: 1st IEEE International Workshop on Broadband Convergence Networks (BcN) (2006)
3. Jennings, B., Van der Meer, S., Balasubramaniam, S., Botvich, D.: Towards Autonomic Management of Communications Networks. IEEE Communications Magazine 45(10), 112–121 (2007)
4. Guerrero, A., Villagrá, A.V., Vergara, J., Berrocal, J.: Ontology-Based Integration of Management Behaviour and Information Definitions Using SWRL and OWL. In: Schön-wälder, J., Serrat, J. (eds.) DSOM 2005. LNCS, vol. 3775, pp. 12–23. Springer, Heidelberg (2005)
5. Wong, A., Ray, P., Parameswaran, N., Strassner, J.: Ontology Mapping for the Interoperability Problem in Network Management. IEEE journal on selected areas in communications 23(10) (2005)
6. Serrano, M., Serrat, J., Strassner, J.: Ontology-Based Reasoning for Supporting Context-Aware Services on Autonomic Networks. In: ICC (2007)
7. Ramakrishna, V., Eustice, K., Reiher, P.: Negotiating Agreements Using Policies in Ubiquitous Computing Scenarios. In: The Proceedings of the IEEE International Conference on Service-Oriented Computing and Applications (2007)
8. Sarangan, V., Chen, J.: Comparative Study of Protocols for Dynamic Service Negotiation in Next Generation Internet. IEEE Communications Magazine - Special issue on Network & Service Management Series (2006)
9. Paschke, A., Bichler, M.: Knowledge Representation Concepts for Automated SLA Management. In: CoRR (2006)
10. Koumoutsos, G., Thramboulidis, K.: Towards a Knowledge-Base for Building Complex, Proactive and Service-Oriented E-negotiation Systems. In: MCeTech (2008)
11. The Ontology Alignment Source, http://www.atl.lmco.com/projects/ontology/
12. Kephart, J., Das, R.: Achieving Self-Management via Utility Functions. IEEE Internet Computing 11(1), 40–48 (2007)

Author Index

Lecture Notes in Computer Science

Sublibrary 5: Computer Communication Networks and Telecommunications

Vol. 4479: I.F. Akyildiz, R. Sivakumar, E. Ekici, J.C.d. Oliveira, J. McNair (Eds.), NETWORKING 2007. Ad Hoc and Sensor Networks, Wireless Networks, Next Generation Internet. XXVII, 1252 pages. 2007.

Vol. 4465: T. Chahed, B. Tuffin (Eds.), Network Control and Optimization. XIII, 305 pages. 2007.

Vol. 4458: J. Löffler, M. Klann (Eds.), Mobile Response. X, 163 pages. 2007.

Vol. 4427: S. Uhlig, K. Papagiannaki, O. Bonaventure (Eds.), Passive and Active Network Measurement. XI, 274 pages. 2007.

Vol. 4396: J. García-Vidal, L. Cerdà-Alabern (Eds.), Wireless Systems and Mobility in Next Generation Internet. IX, 271 pages. 2007.

Vol. 4373: K.G. Langendoen, T. Voigt (Eds.), Wireless Sensor Networks. XIII, 358 pages. 2007.

Vol. 4357: L. Buttyán, V.D. Gligor, D. Westhoff (Eds.), Security and Privacy in Ad-Hoc and Sensor Networks. X, 193 pages. 2006.

Vol. 4347: J. López (Ed.), Critical Information Infrastructures Security. X, 286 pages. 2006.

Vol. 4325: J. Cao, I. Stojmenovic, X. Jia, S.K. Das (Eds.), Mobile Ad-hoc and Sensor Networks. XIX, 887 pages. 2006.

Vol. 4320: R. Gotzhein, R. Reed (Eds.), System Analysis and Modeling: Language Profiles. X, 229 pages. 2006.

Vol. 4311: K. Cho, P. Jacquet (Eds.), Technologies for Advanced Heterogeneous Networks II. XI, 253 pages. 2006.

Vol. 4272: P. Havinga, M. Lijding, N. Meratnia, M. Wegdam (Eds.), Smart Sensing and Context. XI, 267 pages. 2006.

Vol. 4269: R. State, S. van der Meer, D. O'Sullivan, T. Pfeifer (Eds.), Large Scale Management of Distributed Systems. XIII, 282 pages. 2006.

Vol. 4268: G. Parr, D. Malone, M. Ó Foghlú (Eds.), Autonomic Principles of IP Operations and Management. XIII, 237 pages. 2006.

Vol. 4267: A. Helmy, B. Jennings, L. Murphy, T. Pfeifer (Eds.), Autonomic Management of Mobile Multimedia Services. XIII, 257 pages. 2006.

Vol. 4240: S.E. Nikoletseas, J.D.P. Rolim (Eds.), Algorithmic Aspects of Wireless Sensor Networks. X, 217 pages. 2006.

Vol. 4238: Y.-T. Kim, M. Takano (Eds.), Management of Convergence Networks and Services. XVIII, 605 pages. 2006.

Vol. 4235: T. Erlebach (Ed.), Combinatorial and Algorithmic Aspects of Networking. VIII, 135 pages. 2006.

Vol. 4217: P. Cuenca, L. Orozco-Barbosa (Eds.), Personal Wireless Communications. XV, 532 pages. 2006.

Vol. 4195: D. Gaiti, G. Pujolle, E.S. Al-Shaer, K.L. Calvert, S. Dobson, G. Leduc, O. Martikainen (Eds.), Autonomic Networking. IX, 316 pages. 2006.

Vol. 4124: H. de Meer, J.P.G. Sterbenz (Eds.), Self-Organizing Systems. XIV, 261 pages. 2006.

Vol. 4104: T. Kunz, S.S. Ravi (Eds.), Ad-Hoc, Mobile, and Wireless Networks. XII, 474 pages. 2006.

Vol. 4074: M. Burmester, A. Yasinsac (Eds.), Secure Mobile Ad-hoc Networks and Sensors. X, 193 pages. 2006.

Vol. 4033: B. Stiller, P. Reichl, B. Tuffin (Eds.), Performability Has its Price. X, 103 pages. 2006.

Vol. 4026: P.B. Gibbons, T. Abdelzaher, J. Aspnes, R. Rao (Eds.), Distributed Computing in Sensor Systems. XIV, 566 pages. 2006.

Vol. 4003: Y. Koucheryavy, J. Harju, V.B. Iversen (Eds.), Next Generation Teletraffic and Wired/Wireless Advanced Networking. XVI, 582 pages. 2006.

Vol. 3996: A. Keller, J.-P. Martin-Flatin (Eds.), Self-Managed Networks, Systems, and Services. X, 185 pages. 2006.

Vol. 3976: F. Boavida, T. Plagemann, B. Stiller, C. Westphal, E. Monteiro (Eds.), NETWORKING 2006. Networking Technologies, Services, and Protocols; Performance of Computer and Communication Networks; Mobile and Wireless Communications Systems. XXVI, 1276 pages. 2006.

Vol. 3970: T. Braun, G. Carle, S. Fahmy, Y. Koucheryavy (Eds.), Wired/Wireless Internet Communications. XIV, 350 pages. 2006.

Vol. 3964: M.Ü. Uyar, A.Y. Duale, M.A. Fecko (Eds.), Testing of Communicating Systems. XI, 373 pages. 2006.

Vol. 3961: I. Chong, K. Kawahara (Eds.), Information Networking. XV, 998 pages. 2006.

Vol. 3912: G.J. Minden, K.L. Calvert, M. Solarski, M. Yamamoto (Eds.), Active Networks. VIII, 217 pages. 2007.

Vol. 3883: M. Cesana, L. Fratta (Eds.), Wireless Systems and Network Architectures in Next Generation Internet. IX, 281 pages. 2006.

Vol. 3868: K. Römer, H. Karl, F. Mattern (Eds.), Wireless Sensor Networks. XI, 342 pages. 2006.

Vol. 3854: I. Stavrakakis, M. Smirnov (Eds.), Autonomic Communication. XIII, 303 pages. 2006.

Vol. 3813: R. Molva, G. Tsudik, D. Westhoff (Eds.), Security and Privacy in Ad-hoc and Sensor Networks. VIII, 219 pages. 2005.

Vol. 3462: R. Boutaba, K.C. Almeroth, R. Puigjaner, S. Shen, J.P. Black (Eds.), NETWORKING 2005. XXX, 1483 pages. 2005.